The
Desert
Garden

The Desert Garden

A PRACTICAL GUIDE

Irina Springuel

The American University in Cairo Press
Cairo • New York

Dar el Kutub No. 22571/06
ISBN-10: 977 416 021 5
ISBN-13: 978 977 416 021 9

1 2 3 4 5 6   12 11 10 09 08 07 06

Designed by Sally Boylan/AUC Press Design Center
Printed in Egypt

For my grandchildren
Zachary and Leila-Natalie

Contents

Foreword by Ibrahim Abouleish   ix

Acknowledgments   xi

Introduction   xiii

1. The Egyptian Deserts and Oases   1

    The Eastern Desert   2

    The Western Desert   7

       Siwa Oasis   9

       Kharga Oasis   11

       Dungul Oasis   13

2. The Nile Valley around Aswan   15

3. Ecology of Desert Plants and Adaptation to Aridity   18

4. Types of Desert Gardens   25

    Small private gardens   26

    Hotel gardens   29

    Gardens at historical sites   32

    Plants in the new desert settlements

       and alongside roads and streets   36

5. Gardens for Education and Research   37

    School gardens   37

    University gardens   39

Contents

6. Collection and Propagation of Desert Plants 44

    Availability of propagules 45

    Storing seeds 47

    Pre-sowing treatment of seeds 48

    Seed germination 48

    Vegetative propagation 49

    Containers and soil used 53

    Protection of seedlings 54

7. Irrigation Techniques 56

    Drip or trickle irrigation system 57

    Subsurface irrigation 58

    Buried clay pot irrigation 58

    Vertical pipe method of irrigation 61

8. Plant Descriptions 64

    Trees and shrubs 64

    Shrubs 117

    Herbs and grasses 132

Afterword 139

Notes 142

Bibliography 148

Index 153

Foreword

The desert, which accounts for 96 percent of our intriguing country, Egypt, is usually perceived as a dead and hostile place, but is it really? Bedouins call the desert "Sea without water,"or *bahr bela ma'*, and have known for centuries that it is teeming with life, but why are we often blind to all this beauty?

The distinguished scientist and philosopher Goethe once said that he could learn more traveling from Weimar to Erfurt than most people do while traveling the world, through conscious observation and attention to detail. Following his example, it is easy to see that the desert harbors a wealth of life that usually remains overlooked. Just look properly, and with a little patience, perseverance and due diligence, a whole variety of plants and animals will appear, even to the untrained observer.

Why is all this beauty so concealed? To survive in the unique environmental conditions of the desert, plants and animals are formed to cope with the lack of water. During periods when rain is very rare or even absent, they use survival techniques, such as shedding leaves, that have the effect of reducing their visibility. Whenever water becomes available though, as in occasional quite violent rainstorms, the desert blossoms for a short period of time and becomes a magnificent and colorful garden.

Such is the charm and splendor of life in the desert that it has inspired many artists, scientists and other visitors and has stimulated films like *The Living Desert*. The only prerequisite for discovering the diversity of desert life is true interest and the willingness to pay attention to detail.

Lack of knowledge about the natural treasures of Egypt, and a certain lack of care, have endangered many of the plants and animals that live in the desert, because their environment is being poisoned or destroyed. To save them, we have to rediscover the natural heritage this country provides for us, learn to protect it, and teach all of this to our children. By bringing native plants into our parks and gardens, a valuable contribution can be made to this noble goal.

With this book, Dr. Irina Springuel makes a real contribution to the protection of our environment. Through the use of native Egyptian desert plants in our gardens and parks, and by introducing our children to the living wonders around us, curiosity can be stimulated and learning initiated. Opening our children's eyes and training their attention to detail will be valuable both for them and the country at large.

I hope that you will have as much pleasure reading and using this book as I have had, and that you too can start marveling at the wonders nature presents us with in the desert.

Prof. Dr. Ibrahim Abouleish
Founder and President of SEKEM

Acknowledgments

I would like to thank the UNESCO office in Cairo (Mediterranean Programme), Network of Gardens and Landscapes of the Mediterranean for kindly providing financial support enabling me to commission some of the plant drawings.

This book could not been written without the support and encouragement provided by Ahmed Belal and Caryll Faraldi, who revised and checked the text. I extend my sincere thanks to Dr. Mohamed Kassas for providing library facilities, making suggestions, and giving advice on the manuscript.

My visits to the desert garden of Dina Aly inspired me while I was writing this book and I warmly thank her for invaluable practical information on cultivation. I express my appreciation of Marwan El Azzouni for welcoming me to his desert garden and for his useful information.

Walid Belal read part of the draft of this book and made some helpful suggestions. Both Hala Barakat and Fathalla El-Sheikh read the draft manuscript and made some useful comments. Rim Hamdy guided me to some useful sources of information and Osman Ali sent me valuable literature from Sudan. I am thankful to Mohamed El-Hossainy El-Akkad, director of the Agricultural Museum in Doqqi and his staff for many pleasant and informative visits.

My grateful thanks to the following for providing photographs, the map and information for this book: Hala Barakat, BioMap Project EEAA, Center for Documentation of Cultural and Natural Heritage (Cultnat), Egypt, Ahmed Hegazy, Haytham Ibrahim, Rafik Khalil and Dina Aly, Abdel Monem Mekki, Magdi Radi, and Mohamed Gaber Sheded.

I am grateful to Irina Lavrova and Magdy El-Gohary for their plant drawings and to Nadia Kotb, Ludmila Korovina, and Irina El-Sheikh who made several illustrations for this book.

Introduction

The idea of the desert garden appeals to many people who enjoy creating their own gardens or visiting others. The interest in desert plants stems in part from the peculiar appearance of cacti and succulents which has created worldwide popularity. Cacti, which originated in the American continent, and succulents, many of which came from the Cape region of Africa, have been introduced to almost every part of our planet—as indoor plants in cold climates and outdoor plants in hot areas. This interest has increased the commercial value of such plants, which can be seen for sale in flower shops and garden centers that are mushrooming in Europe and North America. However, not only cacti but other desert plants have very distinctive and attractive features.

There are no constraints on growing indoor succulent plants, provided sufficient heating and light are available. Outdoor desert gardens can only be created in hot, arid climates, and in certain regions of North America desert gardens have become fashionable. However, not much has been published about growing desert plants in North Africa and the Middle East where the climate is the most favorable for creating desert gardens.

Egypt is one of the world's driest countries, with desert composing almost 96 percent of its land. Yet there is a great variety of indigenous trees and shrubs in Egypt with a high economic potential which can grow in diverse habitats and consume little water while being cultivated; some plants can also grow on the water edge and survive long inundation periods. The restoration of desert habitats by planting indigenous desert plants with high market value has been carried out in Wadi Allaqi Biosphere Reserve in the south of the Eastern Desert during the last two decades. However, the aesthetic as well as the functional value of the native plants should also be taken into consideration in rural and urban planning. Trees, in particular, can provide both decoration and shade if planted along roads and streets. The cultivation of indigenous plants could also benefit the tourist industry, which is vital to the Egyptian economy.

In Egypt a wealth of ancient information on plants and their uses has been recorded in hieroglyphic inscriptions found in tombs and temples and in papyrus documents. In addition, Egypt is the only country where an abundance of dry plants and fragments have been well preserved for more than three thousand years. Discovered in pharaonic tombs, these ancient plant remains are conserved in several museums and specialized collections. Walls in a number of tombs and temples are decorated with landscapes showing wildlife, and scenes of activities such as hunting, fishing, and harvesting. Wall paintings and reliefs also show ancient gardens and the plants growing in them as an important component of everyday life, as well as the sacred gardens of the temples. All this arouses curiosity and interest in the natural Egyptian wildlife, past and present.

Marie-Luise Gothein's book *A History of Garden Art*[1] begins with a description of ancient Egyptian garden design. She believes that early and important development in garden cultivation began in ancient Egypt and gives a most delightful description of the garden of Meten, an official and high priest, who lived more than 4,500 years ago. "If we look at the beautiful regular plan, the fine alternation of trees, planted with prudent forethought, the elegant shape of the sunk ponds, the judiciously disposed buildings in the garden—we recognize with astonishment that we here have a formal garden in an advanced state of development on the very threshold of our history. Rhythm, symmetry, and a happy combination of elegance and utility—a blend often desired in later days of hope and struggle—these have been fully attained, and with them a delight in quiet communion with Nature, expressing as she does the sense of beauty in orderliness."

The Greeks and Romans admired ancient Egyptian gardens, some of whose elements, such as symmetry and terracing, subsequently became standard in garden design (Wilkinson 1998). However, at present the ancient monuments and historical sites throughout Egypt, from Al-Alamein on the Mediterranean north coast to Abu Simbel in the far south are surrounded by non-native plants, among which the Indian Laurel, Australian Pine (casuarina), and Eucalyptus trees are dominant, and have unfavorable aspects. Hardly any indigenous species are to be found at Al-Alamein, the most renowned World War II battleground in Egypt, and while bougainvillea gives a decorative appearance to the cemeteries, it is not native to Egypt. Egyptian Nubia was noted for its abundant palm trees, but the Abu Simbel temples, now relocated on the shores of Lake Nasser, are mainly surrounded by introduced trees, including the ubiquitous Indian Laurel, and the Australian casuarina, and eucalyptus. This surprises many visitors, who would like to see a natural environment with indigenous plants. The historic value of archaeological sites would increase if their environs supported plants that traditionally belong to such areas, e.g., several kinds of acacia trees, palms native to Egypt (*doum* and *argoun*), the Egyptian plum, and the Christ-thorn tree.

Attractive indigenous trees providing good shade, particularly tamarisk, are grown in some locations along the Mediterranean north coast and in the Nile Valley, where local people value their properties and uses, such as firewood. Olive trees and date palms are cultivated for commercial purposes throughout Egypt; recently, these trees have become important features in landscaped public gardens (an excellent example is the new Al-Azhar garden in Islamic Cairo) and are being planted along main roads, such as the Cairo-Alexandria Desert Highway.

Restoration of habitats around the monuments and historical sites can assist in dealing with some of the environmental problems facing such areas. For example, the planting of desert trees around monuments located in exposed desert sites would decrease soil erosion, while protecting monuments from wind erosion and improving drainage through water uptake and transpiration. In addition, the monuments and archaeological sites of the Nile Valley and Lake Nasser could be surrounded by indigenous Nile Valley plants, such as tamarisk and some acacia species, which can withstand both drought and prolonged inundation.

In hotel gardens managers have faced many problems with introduced plants through lack of information and guidelines for suitable planting. This is particularly so in the Red Sea recreational areas, where salinity and limited fresh water supply have created difficulties in the establishment of green areas. Cultivation of native salt-tolerant and drought-resistant plants, including some acacia and tamarisk species, the toothbrush tree, caper shrubs and the common fig, could help to solve such problems. With increasing awareness of environmental issues and promotion of ecotourism, eco-lodges have been created in different parts of Egypt. Landscape preservation and restoration are important components in establishing such eco-lodges. The cultivation of indigenous plants, many of which are threatened species, would create small islands of wildlife, contributing to biodiversity protection in Egypt.

Introduction

The idea of writing this book initially developed in response to requests from managers of hotels and tourist resorts on the Red Sea for advice on plants that were low water consumers, after receiving large water bills for garden irrigation. Subsequently, some local authorities in Upper Egypt were searching for the most suitable plants for gardening and landscaping; and individuals interested in nature were looking for native Egyptian plants for their gardens. The rising general and specialized interest in the cultivation of native plants stimulated the author to write this book.

Its purpose is to encourage people of different backgrounds (scientists, educators, hotel managers, tourism and antiquities authorities, members of the general public, and others interested in nature) to establish their own gardens where indigenous plants are either the dominant component or a small segment of the garden.

The content of this book is based on scientific information, though the scientific terminology has been simplified to be more comprehensible to the general reader. However, some specific botanical terms are still used, with explanations either in the text or in the end notes. The common English names of the plants are used for preference, with Latin names given in brackets. Some plants growing in the wild have only local names and do not have English names, while some are given different names by different desert tribes.[2]

The book begins with an outline of the vegetation of the Eastern and Western Egyptian deserts and the Nile Valley in order to provide readers with general information on the habitats where most of the plants described in this book are found in the wild. The Sinai and Gebel Elba mountain areas are very rich in floristic diversity and endemic species but are not within the scope of this book.

Knowing how the plants adapt to the dry conditions prevailing in arid lands can help in the maintenance of garden and alleviate concern, for example, about a plant's slow growth, and allay panic if plants shed their leaves or if a soft, smooth, young plant changes to a leafless spiny one when mature. Adaptation to aridity is covered in Chapter 3.

Indigenous plants can contribute to a great variety of gardens and landscaping. In Chapters 4 and 5, recommendations are given for selecting suitable plants according to the type of garden. Nevertheless, the actual arrangement of the plants has to be decided by the owner or garden manager for each specific garden, depending on factors such as the amount of land available, and the surrounding scenery and environment.

For readers new to gardening, Chapter 6 explains how to cultivate the plants and where they can obtain the plant material for propagation. Guidance on the propagation of indigenous plants is based mainly on the author's experience in growing some local desert plants in Aswan and in Wadi Allaqi Biosphere Reserve in the far south of the Eastern Desert, though some information was gathered from Internet web-sites and published material. This chapter was written basically for people who wish to start their own small garden in the simplest way without spending too much time and money. Yet it should be noted that establishing irrigation, as described in Chapter 7, requires both effort and some expenditure. Readers can select the most appropriate way to water their plants from the different types of irrigation techniques described in this chapter.

The selection of plants for the desert garden is an important element of this book and is dealt with in Chapter 8. Indigenous desert plants are favored. It has not been established if the date palm, olive, and oleander are native to Egypt, but these plants have a long history of cultivation in Egypt. The same is true for the downy thorn apple *(Datura)* which originated in Central America but was introduced into Egypt a long time ago and has since naturalized. Oleander is already widely used in landscape gardening, but often misplaced, without taking into consideration that all its parts are extremely poisonous. Most of the plants described in this book are perennials, long-living plants, which are easier to deal with than short-living annuals. Once established, perennials will flourish in the garden for many years while annuals take more gardening effort and need to be newly planted every year.

Plants are listed in this book according to their growth forms, such as trees, shrubs, herbs and grasses. Yet the plasticity of the growth forms, which is common in many native plants, should be taken into consideration; for depending on the environment, water availability, and the impact of humans, some plants may become either trees or shrubs.

Simple descriptions are given of plants, highlighting characteristics of specific interest to gardeners. Illustrations are provided for each plant to enable easy recognition even by a non-specialist. The Egyptian flora is rich in plants that have a high potential for both ornament and use. This book deals only with a small proportion of such plants, about whose propagation at least some information is available.

1

The Egyptian Deserts and Oases

Although 96 percent of the Egyptian land area is desert, the environment in this desert varies considerably from the north to the south and from the west to the east. The Western (or Libyan) Desert, extending west of the river Nile to the Libyan border, is sandy; while the Eastern (or Arabian) Desert, extending east of the Nile to Sinai, is rocky. The southern part of the Egyptian desert is also known as the Nubian Desert. Sinai Peninsula has a variety of landforms and habitats, ranging from the Mediterranean coastal plain on the north through the central gravelly plateau to the high mountains in the south, rising about 2000 meters above sea level (ASL), of which the highest point is Mount Catherine at 2,641 meters ASL.

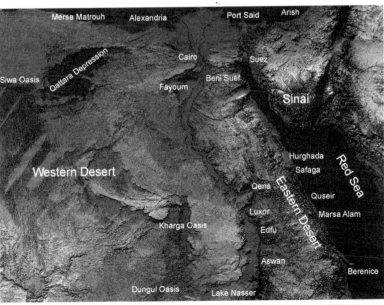

Figure 1: Map of Egypt showing areas described in the book. Courtesy of BioMap Project EEAA.

Common to both the Eastern and the Western Deserts is the aridity, which increases from north to south following the decreasing level of rainfall. However, the annual rainfall alone does not explain the spatial variation in plant distribution. Plants do not take water directly from the rain, but from the soil which stores rainwater and supports the plant growth. The moisture available for plant growth depends on variations in atmospheric moisture, land surface and relief, soil characteristics, hydrology, and air temperature, which affects evaporation. The most important factor in determining aridity is the temporal and spatial unreliability of rainfall, which is least reliable in the southern part of the Egyptian desert where rainless episodes may extend for several years. This contrasts with the northern part of the desert, where rain occurs more regularly in the winter period despite the amount of rainfall being negligible in some years.

The Eastern Desert

The Eastern Desert is the rocky plateau east of the Nile extending to the chain of hills along the Red Sea. In the north it is a narrow semi-desert belt along the Mediterranean coast, and the desert proceeds south to the border with Sudan. The Eastern Desert comprises three main rock formations: limestone in the north, sandstone desert in the south and the basement complex, a regional mass of Achaean metamorphic crystalline rocks and igneous intrusions, in the east. In its southern part the Nubia sandstone appears on the surface as a great plateau overlooking the Nile Valley. This plateau extends eastwards to the backbone of the desert (the Red Sea Hills with their igneous, metamorphic, and sedimentary rocks). Sometimes, enclaves of Nubia sandstone appear to the east of the Red Sea–Nile basin divide, such as the Abraq area.

The main topographic feature of this desert is the drainage system, which dissects the rocky plateau and forms the ephemeral rivers, whose dry beds are locally called wadis.[3] The chain of the Red Sea Hills forms the divide, which directs the drainage eastward to the Red Sea and westward to the River Nile.

The rainfall in the north part of the Eastern Desert (near and to the north of Cairo) is about 30 mm annually with marked temporal and spatial variations. Even such a small amount of rainfall supports the diffuse perennial vegetation, which is scattered on the desert plain. With decreasing rainfall, also increasing in its unpredictability, toward the south (almost nil in some years) the distribution of vegetation becomes contracted, its growth restricted to the drainage lines in the wadis. Here, the actual moisture collected in the wadi system, which drains the extensive rocky plateau, exceeds the annual amount of rainfall and supports the perennial plants, particularly trees, which are deeply rooted in the wadi-fill deposits.

Decades can pass without a drop of water falling in the southern part of the desert, but on very rare occasions, the dry wadi is converted into a violent river.[4] When a torrent comes so suddenly, people cannot prepare for it and it becomes very destructive, tearing away or destroying everything in its path. One such event was observed in Wadi Aggag near Aswan in 1980, which destroyed many houses, the road, and the industrial railway connecting Aswan with the mines in the Aggag area.

Desert trees and shrubs growing in wadis have a special adaptation to survive both long drought and violent flood, by rooting themselves deeply into the wadi terrace. Despite the tree species growing in the Eastern Desert being limited in number, they play the crucial role of backbone plants in the structure of desert plant communities. The distribution of these species is controlled by their ecological range as well as the land-use history and area of the plants' distribution.

Of the three acacia species, *Acacia tortilis* subsp. *raddiana* is widely distributed in the wadis throughout the Eastern Desert, successfully coexisting with the two other acacias (*A. tortilis* subsp. *tortilis* and *A. ehrenbergiana*). Growth of the umbrella thorn (*A. tortilis* subsp. *tortilis*), which is a drought-tolerant plant but less drought resistant than *A. ehrenbergiana*, is restricted to the southern and eastern part of the desert. Very rarely have both species been observed growing together. Both subspecies of *Acacia tortilis* (*raddiana* and *tortilis*) are trees with an umbrella-shaped crown, the former being rounded and the latter flattened. However, it is not always easy to find trees with crowns of a natural shape. Trees tend to be shaped by the Bedouins carrying out *ewak*, i.e., the cutting of young branches as fodder for their goats and sheep when no other grazing plants are available.[5]

Salam (Acacia ehrenbergiana) usually has the appearance of a shrub; it sometimes grows as a tree with a single trunk, but this is very rare. It tends to be heavily browsed, especially by camels. Browsing causes the very peculiar shape of this plant, which resembles a flat-topped umbrella. Camels and even goats can easily reach the outside branches and heavily browse them, but cannot reach the branches further inside; these inside branches grow freely, rising above the middle of the smaller outside branches and forming this curious shape.

In the northern part of the Eastern Desert, there are fewer trees than in its south. A few instances of umbrella thorn can be seen there, as well as scattered populations of acacia *(Acacia raddiana)*. Most probably, the majority of the trees have been cut down for firewood and charcoal, because the north of Egypt is more densely populated and in close proximity to large cities such as Cairo, where for millennia there has been a demand for perennial woody plants to use as firewood.

The Egyptian plum tree *(Balanites aegyptiaca)* has the northern limit of its geographical distribution in the Nubian Desert and grows abundantly only in the southern part of the Egyptian desert. Notably rich in Egyptian plum are the wadis close to the Red Sea Hills, such as Wadi Gemal. A relatively undisturbed population of this tree is present in the upstream part of Wadi Allaqi where it is associated with acacias and other woody species, including *tagart* bush *(Maerua crassifolia), Capparis decidua,* Christ-thorn *(Ziziphus spina-christi)* and toothbrush tree *(Salvadora persica),* whose distribution within the Eastern Desert is both patchy and very limited. Both wadis have been declared conservation areas, a status which may help to protect the biodiversity in these most spectacular habitats.

The toothbrush tree is a most interesting plant in the plasticity of its growth form: it usually grows as a shrub, but, if not disturbed, it can grow into a tree; in rocky habitats, it clumps on rocks as do lianas. When the shrubs grow at the bottom of a wadi, they often form hillocks that are a few meters high. The leaf-fall of the shrub itself and debris of other plants brought by run-off water and wind accumulate inside and beside the shrub, completely covering its base. With age, the entire shrubs can become covered by deposits, and only a few live branches are seen on the top of such hillocks, as occurs in Wadi Gemal. In the mid-stream part of Wadi Allaqi the high fossil hillocks of the toothbrush tree are above eight meters in height and most probably around 800 years in age. Live ones still exist in the wadi's upstream part.

It is likely that *Salvadora persica*'s appearance as a shrub has anthropogenic causes. The woody branches of this shrub have been used as toothbrushes by the local Bedouins of the Eastern Desert since their long history of inhabiting this area began. In addition the shrub has commercial value, as an extract of this plant is added to at least one brand of toothpaste. The leaves can also provide fodder for livestock when other feed is not available. Even the dry leaves buried in hillocks are eaten by wild animals. Throughout Wadi Allaqi, Dorcas gazelles have been seen eating the dry leaves on the fossil hillocks of the toothbrush tree.

This plant produces fruits that look like berries with a small round seed inside. We have collected these seeds but could not succeed in germinating them either in laboratory or nursery conditions. The fleshy fruits have a sweet taste with a slightly piney flavor. Once, when we were forced to stay a few days without sufficient food in the upstream part of Wadi Allaqi on the Sudanese border because our car had broken down, we added some other desert plants to our diet. These include the leaves of *hommad (Rumex)*, similar to spinach but with an acidic savor, good for soup, *Sonchus* leaves which we ate as a salad, Egyptian plum fruits, which have a bitter-sweet taste, and these toothbrush tree fruits, providing a nice dessert for our meals.

Another interesting plant is the tamarisk shrub *(Tamarix nilotica)*, which is a relict of the tamarisk population in the southern part of the Eastern Desert, indicating the moist conditions prevailing there in the past. Evidence for this is provided by fossil plant remains present in silt hillocks occurring in the middle—now the driest—part of Wadi Allaqi. A relict community of tamarisk still grows in the upstream part of Wadi Haimur, a tributary of Wadi Allaqi, where ground water occurs close to the surface. It also grows in Wadi Qena in the Eastern Desert, which runs parallel to the Nile. Fossil hillocks of tamarisk are present here on the wadi terraces, while live individuals grow in the bottom.

The trees and shrubs described above are the keystone of the vegetation forming the permanent plant cover. It is not within the scope of this book to describe all of the important plants growing in the desert, but the picture of the Eastern Desert would not be complete without mention of a few more plants that are important for the livelihood of the nomadic population still inhabiting the desert.

Solenostemma arghel is a low shrub growing in rocky habitats, usually in small wadi tributaries in the southern part of the Eastern Desert. This plant is extremely important for the Bedouin people who live here because it is well known for its medicinal value; it is used locally and sold to market traders in the Egyptian urban areas where it is known as *hargal*. It is also an extremely beautiful and delightfully fragrant plant with white flowers attracting many pollinating insects and birds.

The only naturally surviving population of *Cymbopogon proximus*, the grass locally known as *halfa barr*, is found in the southern part of Egypt's Eastern Desert on the border with Sudan. It is a threatened plant in Egypt, most probably as the result of overexploitation because of its extremely important medicinal value, as well as being a popular refreshing drink in Upper Egypt.

Those who have been lucky enough to travel through the desert after rain will never forget its beauty, when the annual plants grow and transform the barren desert into the most beautiful variegated land. Yellow, blue, green, and white are the main colors of the desert in bloom, an extremely rare but outstanding and memorable event for lovers of nature. There are yellow carpets of *Cotula cinerea* and *Pulicaria incisa*, with blue patches of *Lupinus digitatus* and *Fagonia indica*, and green spots of small succulent *Zygophyllum simplex*, which spread over the ground; the convolvulus with white and blue flowers adds to the carpet's ornamentation. (This is an occasion when you may have the chance to drink 'desert tea,' which Bedouins serve by adding *shaay gabali (Pulicaria incisa)* to boiling water.)

It is interesting to note that yellow flowers predominate in desert plants. Blue and white flowers are common, but plants with red flowers are very rare and can be seen only in the northern part of the desert. The perennial plants *Cleome chrysantha, Cleome droserifolia, Senna italica* and *Senna alexandrina*—all of which have yellow flowers—add to the desert's blooming later on, when the annuals are producing their seeds and completing their brief life cycle. *Senna alexandrina*, which is still better known by its previous name *Cassia senna*, is a medicinal plant that is not only locally used but also collected to be sold in markets. The raw material from this plant is used in the pharmaceutical industry in Egypt as well as exported.

Among the rocks in small wadis, which are the upstream tributaries, a fortunate observer can see the annuals *Cleome paradoxa, Sesamum alatum, Gisekia pharnaceoides, Anticharis linearis*, and *Anticharis arabica* all of which are very rare plants in the Egyptian flora.

In the northern part of the Eastern Desert there are many succulent plants of the salt-loving family Chenopodiaceae, such as *Haloxylon salicornicum*, and *agram (Anabasis articulata)*. They are both small evergreen shrubs with scale (i.e., minute leaves) and small flowers. Their very attractive fruits with diaphanous wings are of a greenish-yellow to light brown hue in the former and off-white to soft pink in the latter. A related plant is white saksaul (*Haloxylon persicum* from Sinai) which is very rare, but of special interest for cultivation because it grows as a tree. Another interesting shrub with tiny and soon deciduous leaves (i.e., falling soon after they appear), small flowers, and a large eye-catching nut is *arta (Calligonum poly-gonoides* subsp. *comosum*) from the family Polygonaceae. A very graceful perennial is white broom *(Retama raetam)*, a small legume shrub, that is densely covered by white flowers with purplish tips. Low shrubs, *Convolvulus hystrix* with blue flowers and *Convolvulus lanatus* with pink-ish-white flowers add color to the desert landscape.

The Western Desert

The Western Desert is a slightly undulating plateau west of the River Nile, which extends to the Libyan border, and gently slopes from south to north toward the Mediterranean Sea. It covers almost two-thirds of the entire Egyptian land surface. Glimpsed from above (as in air-photos, satellite images) it appears to be a very homogeneous area covered by yellow sand-sheet with some dark spots, which a closer look reveals as rock outcrops, depressions, and cliff edges. The main rock formation is a triangle of lime-stone in the north with its narrow end pointing south along the Nile.[6] The Nubia sandstone formation covers the south part of the Western Desert. Large areas of the desert surface are covered by a compacted layer of peb-bles. Soft sand particles are eroded by the wind leaving pebbles and gravel on the surface of the sand sheet. The sand is deposited in areas where wind velocity decreases and forms sand dunes that can reach a height of above 100 meters in some places. In the southern part of the desert the general flatness is interrupted by outcrops of basement rocks, the larger of which is Gebel Uweinat, rising up to 1893 meters above sea level in the south-ern corner of the Egyptian Western Desert and extending into Libya and Sudan. The sandstone plateau Gilf Kebir, rising about 600 meters above the surrounding plain in the southern part of the desert, is another percep-tible relief characteristic. However, the most noticeable landscape features are depressions that form a chain running parallel to the Nile in the mid-dle of the Western Desert. The main depressions in order of size, from largest to smallest, are Qattara, Farafra, Kharga, Bahariya, Fayoum, Siwa, Dakhla, and Wadi Natrun. The depths of the depressions vary, the lowest point being 133 meters below sea level in the Qattara depression with the highest 113 meters above sea level at Bahariya.

The northern (coastal) part of the Western Desert annually receives about 50 mm of rain, but in some years it can be less. However, only a nar-row strip of land along the Mediterranean receives considerable rain. The southern part of the Western Desert is hyper-arid. Rain is an even less common event than in the Eastern Desert; it may happen only once in decades. Nevertheless, when it does occur, the rainwater quickly penetrates the soft sand to a depth beyond the root zone. The seeds of only a few plants succeed in germinating, these usually being the ephemerals with very short life cycles. Surprisingly, in such a dry area are a few large solitary acacias, which are believed to be several hundred years old and relicts of pluvial episodes in the desert history. However, close to the Mediterranean coast acacias are more abundant, although restricted to the Qattara Depression where they form close canopy groves (Bornkamm and Kehl 1989; Boulos and Barakat 1998).

The hot summer (sometimes above 50°C) and the extreme daily temperature fluctuations in winter (from above 30°C in the day to below zero at night), contribute to harsh conditions for plant growth. In such an environment, plant life is confined to the most favorable habitats, namely depressions and hills rising a few hundred meters above the surrounding desert.

In the large depressions, oases were formed where artesian water reached the surface. In the subsequent long history of human settlement the local biota, both plants and animals, were severely affected by humans. Land was transformed into cultivated fields planted with date palms, fruit trees, and vegetables; it is difficult to ascertain what natural vegetation had been there before human interference. There is no shortage of water for the occupants of oases: the problem here is rather its excess, because of the lack of drainage in such depressions. On reaching the surface, the artesian water then drains to the lower level of the oasis floor, where water collects, forming pools or lakes. Because of high evaporation, the salts present in the water accumulate and the lake water becomes saline. Wetlands and salt marshes that form around the lakes are rich in biodiversity and, together with cultivated fields and moving sand dunes, are the main features of inhabited oases.

Even small, uninhabited oases scattered in the southern portion of the Western Desert have had a long history of human exploitation, being important stops for caravan travelers, grazed by domestic animals, and excavated for minerals. However, because of their small size and limited natural resources, no permanent settlements have been established and they have not been cultivated. Such oases shelter natural or semi-natural vegetation and provide refuge for rare species e.g., the *Medemia argun* palm.

Siwa Oasis

One of the remarkable oases of the Western Desert is Siwa Oasis, approximately 300 kilometers south of the Mediterannean coast and 50 kilometers east of the Libyan border. It is home to about 20,000 people, the majority of whom are ethnic Berbers, the true Western Desert indigenous people, who speak a distinct language known as Siwan. Dalrymple Belgrave[7] gave a most delightful description of Siwa Oasis in the 1920s: "These 'Islands of the Blessed'—as they were called by the ancients—are natural depressions in the great Libyan table-land, which are preserved from the inroad of the shifting sand by the high limestone cliffs that surround them, and are made fertile and habitable by a number of sweet water springs. Siwa consists of a little group of oases in a depression about 30 miles long and 6 miles wide, lying 72 feet below the level of the sea, surrounded by a vast barren table-land, parched and featureless where rain rarely falls."

There are approximately eighteen saline lakes in the depression, which differ in size and shape. Small and shallow lakes may dry up in the summer, or shrink considerably. The largest lakes are Birket Maraqi, Birket Siwa, and Birket Zaytun, which are surrounded by layers of salt and brackish marshlands of reeds (*Phragmites* and *Typha*) with tamarisk, *Juncus rigidus, Alhagi maurorum*, and a few other salt-loving plants. Not many plants grow naturally in the oasis and surrounding areas, which is not surprising, taking into consideration the very harsh, almost rainless climate, where the maximum temperature in summer can be 50°C.

However, luxurious gardens growing in the oasis compensate for the sparse natural plant cover. Anyone visiting Siwa in both the past and the present has noted the plentiful date palms and olive trees. Siwa was known to the Dynastic Egyptians as *Sekhet Amit* or the field of date palms (Zahran and Willis 1992).

In her charming book *The Date Palm*, Warda Bircher (1995) made a comment on a curious reference from Pliny's *Natural History*, which stated "the soldiers of Alexander the Great found the Egyptian dates so delicious that many of them choked to death from over-eating." This happened in the fateful autumn of 332 BCE, when the invincible Macedonian general conquered Egypt during one of his campaigns. This followed the well-known visit by Alexander to the Siwa oasis in 331 BCE to consult the famous Oracle of Amun.

The gardens have not changed much in Siwa since the 1920s, when Dalrymple Belgrave wrote: "The gardens consist mainly of date groves with some olive orchards. But among the date palms there are many other trees—figs, pomegranates, pears, peaches, plums, apricots, apples, prickly pears, limes and sweet lemons. The numerous vineyards produce quantities of exceptionally fine grapes which last for several months and are so plentiful that large quantities rot on the branches" (Dalrymple Belgrave 1922).

Dates and olives remain the principal agricultural product in Siwa. The history of the date palm *(Phoenix dactylifera)* is fascinating. Nobody knows with certainty its place of origin, partly because it has been under cultivation since very remote times. It is thought that those palms that grow spontaneously either are escapes from cultivation or have developed from casually dispersed stones. Alternatively, they may be survivors of old, long-abandoned groves in uninhabited oases spread throughout the Sahara desert. There are many records of the cultivation of this plant in ancient Egypt and Mesopotamia, two centers of early civilization. Archaeological evidence indicates that the date palm was already cultivated in the Euphrates Valley by the fifth millennium BCE, "that is about the same epoch as when the first traces of date palm culture appeared in prehistoric Egypt" (Bircher 1995).

The first mummies to be discovered from the Neolithic period were wrapped in mats made from palm leaves. Parts of palms were used in building early dwelling-places and the first known baskets and mats of palm leaves are from the same period. Since the early pharaonic time the palm featured in tomb paintings, reliefs on temple walls, and papyrus scripts, while numerous pharaonic artifacts, as found in tombs, were made from the palm, showing its importance in everyday life. Every part of the tree was used. Its sweet and luscious fruits were eaten both fresh or dried, and fermented into wine,[8] which was not only drunk but also used during the process of mummification to wash the body. As now, liquate was extracted from the trunk of the tree (unfortunately the tree often dies) and left to ferment to be enjoyed as an alcoholic drink. The terminal bud on the top of the palm is delicious, with a taste of celery (Manniche 1999). Traditionally, it has been served to the most important guests, because such a delicacy is consumed at the cost of the tree, which cannot grow without its terminal bud and eventually dies. This custom is still practiced in some North African and Arab countries. The trunks were—and still are—very useful for building, the midrib of the palm leaves used to make furniture, the fronds for thatching, basketry, nets and many other items, including sandals found in the Pharaohs' tombs. Dates are also important in traditional medicine, for such things as potions, suppositories, unguents, and poultices (Manniche 1999; Springuel *et al.* 2005).

Kharga Oasis

Kharga Oasis lies in the middle of the Western Desert, in the southern part of a chain of depressions. It is approximately 220 kilometers by road southwest of Assiut and about 210 kilometers west of Luxor in the Nile Valley.

Kharga is a long, narrow depression, some 185 kilometers from north to south and between 15 and 30 kilometers from west to east. Its elevation ranges from 18 meters below sea level to 86 meters above sea level (Abu Al-Izz 1971). The water supply, as in most oases, comes from natural springs, the water rising to the surface from below, under natural pressure. Artificial wells were bored to tap some of the deeper water-bearing strata. All these springs and wells are situated in depressions and supply water to natural and cultivated plants, which appear as bright green patches within the barren, sand-covered land.

Kharga Oasis has been inhabited since prehistoric times: evidence of human settlements has been discovered by archaeologists at a depth of four meters. Within the oasis are numerous ruins of ancient towns and temples, which testify to its former importance, especially in Roman times when all the oases enjoyed their greatest prosperity (Vivian 2000). Ball (1900), who headed the Geological Survey of Kharga Oasis in 1898, noted the numerous *doum* and date palms, *sont* trees (acacia), tamarisk bushes, bulrushes, *agol (Alhagi graecorum)* prickly bushes, which surrounded the springs and indicated the location of the wells. Kharga differs from Siwa Oasis in that it has been intensively developed, and little is left of its beautiful natural plant cover.

Major C.S. Jarvis, on his arrival in Kharga in 1920, observed, "Three thousand acres of dense palm groves, olives and apricot gardens" irrigated by a great number of wells which were bored to a depth of 60–90 meters. The system of boring wells to a depth of 300 feet was introduced by the Persians during their occupation of Egypt in about 500 BCE (Jarvis 1947).

Early in the nineteenth century (in about 1830), a French engineer Lefèvre (named by locals Aymé Bey) brought several well-boring systems to Kharga. After his death, these were used by the people of Kharga without any consideration as to whether a well was necessary or not. In many cases wells were bored too deep; the flow of water, which could not be checked once it was tapped, drew off the supply from wells on higher ground, and the surplus water formed big lakes that provided excellent breeding grounds for mosquitoes. Mismanagement of water use led to "thousands of acres of good land on the higher levels left entirely without water and a perfect maze of unnecessary wells on lower levels yielding far more than was required, producing swamps and lakes" (Jarvis 1947). The lessons were not learned: two deep boreholes with a depth of about 500 meters were drilled in 1939 and five other deep wells were drilled before 1952, although it is likely that these deep wells did not affect 412 shallow wells that existed in the oasis at this period (Paver and Pretorius 1954).

The author visited Kharga Oasis in 1982 when the artesian water in a few wells still reached the surface under the natural force of pressure. In the traditional scheme of land cultivation, water from the well through the main channel reaches the storage *mahfaz*, which is usually either round or oval in shape. From the storage, water is directed through one or two canals to orchards or fields that are irrigated by networks of small canals. The drainage water forms one stream, which drains to the depression and forms salt ponds surrounded by wetlands. As soon as a depression is filled with water and its ponds enlarged, it affects the surrounding lands, which become saline. At this point the well should be closed and a new location for cultivation found. Decades pass before saline land becomes suitable for reclamation. The rotation of wells and small-scale agriculture was the traditional practice among the the indigenous people of such oases until the 1970s, when the National Company for Reclamation of Oases was initiated.

Artesian water was pumped from deep wells (over 500 meters in depth) to irrigate cultivated fields and supply the domestic needs of the rapidly growing population. At this time, many people were moving to the oasis looking for work and cultivable land. The villages were extended and some developed into towns. Excess water used for irrigation and domestic needs drained to the low-lying lands, where lakes became enlarged and more saline.

Natural vegetation in Kharga Oasis comprises reed swamps and salt marshes surrounding the lakes, similar to Siwa Oasis. There are still date palm groves and dates are economically important in the oasis, but now contribute less to its economy than in the past.

Remains of natural woody growth are found among the cultivated fields and in the village areas. Huge acacia trees (*Acacia tortilis* subsp. *raddiana* and *Acacia nilotica*) grow along the canals, on abandoned lands and in villages. The most conspicuous is the Egyptian plum tree *(Balanites aegyptiaca)*, which grows around the village of Baris lying in the south of the oasis. This tree is very valuable in the livelihood of the rural areas of Kharga Oasis, providing shade at the hottest time of year, fodder for livestock, and fruits for sale. The fruits, which look like dates, are well known for their medicinal value in treating diabetes: the most common way is to soak three to four mature fruits in a glass of water, which is left overnight and the infusion drunk three times during the next day. One large tree can produce about 200 kilograms of fruits, which are sold on the local market and sent to large cities. *Balanites* fruits from Kharga oasis are more valuable than fruits from the Eastern Desert because they are larger and contain more flesh. The wood from this tree is heavy, hard, and strong, and is widely used to make domestic utensils, small farm tools, furniture, and specialist goods. It is a good fuel and also produces high quality charcoal.

Dungul Oasis

Further south of Kharga Oasis are many tiny uninhabited oases scattered in small depressions in the Western Desert. Among the most interesting is the Dungul oasis complex, which consists of two parts. One is the Dungul Oasis and the other is the Dineigil Oasis, the latter being in an unusually high position on the edge of an escarpment. The single date palm on the highest portion of this escarpment is a landmark that can be seen as far away as twenty kilometers on clear days. There are a few small springs with open water surrounded by rushes *(Juncus rigidus)*, while the location of others, which are covered by sand, can be easily detected from the groups of acacias (*A. tortilis* subsp. *raddiana* and *A. ehrenbergiana*) with *doum* and date palms growing nearby. The most fascinating feature is the growth pattern of the *agol* bushes, which occurs in parallel lines on the slope of the escarpment, giving a spectacular zebra-like appearance to the landscape.

The Dungul Oasis is in a low-lying area, which looks like a small wadi. Because rain is very rare in this part of the desert and may occur only once in many years, a few deeply rooted woody perennial plants (mainly tamarisk), supported by underground water, are the permanent inhabitants of such an oasis. Only two grasses (*Imperata cylindrica* and *Desmostachya bipinnata*) were seen by the author during a few visits to this area between 1995 and 2002. This oasis is the kingdom of palms in Egypt, a unique place where three palms, the *doum (Hyphaene thebaica)*, the date *(Phoenix dactylifera)* and *argoun (Medemia argun)* grow together. In Egypt, the argoun grows only in this oasis, and is one of the most intriguing Egyptian species. Täckholm and Drar (1950) assumed that this palm was once abundant in the oases, and even along the banks of the Nile in Upper Egypt, because of the frequent occurrence of its fruits among the offerings in ancient tombs. The fruits of the *Medemia* were last found in Egypt dating from the sixth to the seventh century BCE in the monastery of Epiphanus and in Thebes (Täckholm and Drar 1950). No living *Medemia* plants were recorded in Egypt from that date until this palm was rediscovered in November 1963 at Dungul Oasis (see Boulos 1968). At that time there were seven young (baby) trees growing around the mother plant, which was twelve meters tall.

The palm was also subsequently recorded at another location in the Western Desert in 1964, by Dr. Issawy, who found it at the very small Nakhila Oasis located 200 kilometers west of Aswan. Dr. Issawy observed that five *Medemia* trees had been cut down in this oasis. A similar fate befell the mother tree at Dungul Oasis. In 1998, a joint expedition of German and Egyptian scientists, in which the author participated, observed that this tree had been burned and had had its top cut off (Bornkamm *et al.* 2000). By then, there was only one female tree left in Dungul Oasis, which had produced fruits. A few mature male trees grew in close proximity to the female and about thirty small trees and seedlings were growing in the vicinity. While on an expedition to Dungul in November 2005, William Baker[9] reported that three palms were bearing fruits.

The small, uninhabited oases also provide a refuge for the *doum* palm *(Hyphaene thebaica)* which has recently become threatened in Egypt with other small populations surviving only in the southern Nile Valley.

2

The Nile Valley around Aswan

The River Nile is the main source of fresh water for the entire Egyptian population. It passes through Egypt from south to north almost in the middle of the country. Near Cairo the Nile divides into two branches, with Rosetta on the west and Damietta on the east marking the boundaries of the classic triangular delta shape, and it covers about 22,000 square kilometers of the most fertile and most densely populated land of Egypt. Täckholm (1976) describes the Egyptian landscape of the Nile Delta in the ancient past: "… during the Neolithic and also the pharaonic times [it] had the character of the Sudd region of the present Sudan, a river with marshy shores where huge papyrus thickets offered a splendid abode for hippopotami and crocodiles, for birds and other animals." Her description is based on plant remains found in pharaonic tombs, ancient drawings, and records written on papyrus.

However, with Egypt's increasing population and growing demand for food, most of the Nile Valley, which once was covered by flourishing riverain vegetation, has been converted to cultivated fields. With the gradual conversion of its natural habitats, many species of the Nile valley vegetation have become rare or almost extinct; among these are the well known plants of ancient Egypt, *Cyperus papyrus, Nymphaea lotus* and *Medemia argun* (Täckholm and Drar 1950).

Remains of natural vegetation can be seen along the irrigation canals where the huge grass *Arundo donax* attracts the attention of those who are passing the area. Alluring white flowers of downy thorn apple *(Datura innoxia)* are often seen along the roadsides, in abandoned fields and agricultural lands. Nile acacia trees are still growing along the roads and canals providing shade where cultivators and their animals rest in the midday heat.

15

Those who travel between Luxor and Aswan by boat can see the desert cliff rising on both sides of the river, sometimes just a few meters from the water. On the narrow terraces are some natural plants, the most noticeable being acacias, tamarisk, henna, and *saisaban*; while on the water's edge reeds, with *Mimosa pigra* and *Pluchea dioscoridis* shrubs, provide refuge for water birds. The *doum* palm, which is native to Nubia, is easy to distinguish from the common cultivated date palm by its branching stem and palmate form of leaves.

Further south, the First Cataract Islands at Aswan harbor semi-natural Nile Valley vegetation, a woodland growth which is not known elsewhere in Egypt (Springuel 1981). In an attempt to protect this unique habitat, conservation status was sought and granted in 1986 for two of the First Cataract Islands, Saluga and Ghazel, which have since been protected by Egyptian law.

The relict of a gallery forest formed by acacia trees fringes the winding edges of the islands. Six acacia species inhabited these islands until the early 1990s, when the sole *Acacia arabica* tree was cut down while a huge hotel was being constructed on Ambonati Island, thus causing the extinction of this species from the Egyptian flora.[10] In addition to the abundant Nile acacia, the common desert acacia, *Acacia tortilis* subsp. *raddiana*, grows on the central elevated parts of the islands together with Christ-thorn *(Ziziphus spina-christi)*, while other acacias outline the lower parts closer to the water. *A. laeta*, *A. seyal*, and *Faidherbia albida* are rare species, present in very few other locations in Egypt because the fertile soils of the Nile Valley have been cultivated and habitats have been lost. Some acacias are densely covered by a liana *(Leptadenia arborea)* which gives the fantastic appearance of a tropical forest when you pass by. *Mimosa pigra* shrubs, which look similar to acacias and grow on the water's edge, add to the allure of this habitat. Their delicate off-white flower heads are eye catching, while the peculiar leaves close when they are touched. When in bloom, the exquisite smell of acacia spreads around the islands attracting insects, bees, butterflies, and many birds that feed on and collect the nectar.

South of the town of Aswan, the huge man-made reservoir (Aswan High Dam Lake) has flooded the whole Nubian Nile Valley and deeply penetrated the desert.

Before the construction of the dam in the 1960s, the raised terraces of the Nubian valley were cultivated, mainly with date palms, while the

Nubians' homes were located at the edge of the desert to escape the seasonal river flood. The bright green patches of natural riverain vegetation comprising different acacia species, tamarisk, *doum* palms, and Egyptian plum, caught the attention of travelers who sailed between the First and Second Cataracts on the Nile. Wetlands linking the banks of the Nile provided refuge for migratory and resident birds and probably for Nile crocodiles.

Homes and vegetation were all submerged in the 1970s when the reservoir gradually filled with water extending almost 500 kilometers south of the town of Aswan. Some major pharaonic monuments were rescued and relocated on the high ground, among which are the famed temples of Philae, Abu Simbel, and Kalabsha. Important artifacts providing historical evidence of the flourishing Nubian civilization are displayed in the Nubian Museum in Aswan.

At present the shores of the huge body of water, which obliterated the old Nubian homeland, are linked by a narrow strip of vegetation on which tamarisk flourishes. On the eastern side of the lake, in Wadi Allaqi,[11] a field station was set up in 1990, where experiments in reintroducing the native plants to their habitats are conducted. Visitors can see demonstration farms with Egyptian plum, acacias, hargal *(Solenostemma arghel)*, and some other desert plants, notably those that are endangered, and can obtain propagation material, if available, as well as information on how to grow these plants.

3

Ecology of Desert Plants and Adaptation to Aridity

Water shortage is the main problem in desert environments. The high temperature and low air humidity add to the difficulties for plant growth. Despite its struggle to obtain water, the plant retains only a very small amount. About 90 percent of the water absorbed is lost to the atmosphere in a process called transpiration, through minute surface pores (stomata) on the leaves. Saline soil and heavy grazing exacerbate the harsh desert conditions. Plants have evolved various mechanisms to cope with these ecological pressures.

When one visits the desert during a long rainless period which may last several years, at first glance the area looks uninhabited and inhospitable, without any living organisms. However, with a closer look, one can note the prints of small mammals and reptiles on the bare sand surface. These usually burrow into the ground during the day to avoid the heat and are active at night when the temperature drops. Careful observation will reveal remains of plants either on the surface or partly covered by sand; and with a magnifying glass, many tiny seeds can be discovered, which provide food for many small herbivorous animals.

Yet, visiting the same area after rain, one will be astonished by luxuriant vegetation densely covering the soil surface, which previously was completely bare. This is one of the main peculiarities of the desert vegetation. Plants which germinate from seeds, grow to mature plants, produce seeds, and die in a one-year period, are called annuals. Those which complete their life cycle and succeed in producing seeds in a few weeks, are named ephemerals. What is characteristic of the desert, is that some perennial plants, which usually grow for more than one year in favorable conditions, can succeed in producing seeds in a short period while there is enough water in the soil for the plant growth. The ephemerals, annuals, and some short-lived perennials avoid the worst season of prolonged drought by germinating quickly after the first shower of rain and completing their life cycles within a few weeks or months. Fast-growing when moisture is available, the short-lived plants produce and disperse enormous amounts of tiny seeds that secure the next generation. The seeds lie dormant in the soil seed bank until rain sets off the next cycle, unless they have been destroyed by inappropriate or careless use of the desert, notably by heavy vehicles on safari.

A peculiar feature of some of these plants is their manner of seed dispersal. Many seeds are equipped with dispersal aids, such as long silky hairs, with the seeds resembling parachutes, or wings, which facilitate their distribution by wind over long distances. Because seeds in the soil are often in danger of consumption by many desert rodents, some ephemerals retain their ripened seeds inside the parent plant throughout the dry season. A striking example is the rose of Jericho *(Anastatica hierochuntica)*. When the plant is dry, the naked woody branches curl up into a ball-like shape, where the seeds survive the prolonged dry period. After rain, the branches uncurl and the seeds disperse, ready to germinate.

All over the desert, other than on bare rock, dormant seeds form seed banks in the soil, whose presence is not easily detectable. Accordingly, as soon as irrigation occurs (as for example when a desert garden is being created), plants may begin to grow spontaneously from these seed banks.

Plants that grow continuously in the desert are long-living woody perennials (called xerophytes), which are very efficient in maintaining the water balance, employing many means to obtain water and reduce water loss. To obtain a sufficient amount of water the plants develop an extensive root system which is densely spread through a large area of soil. To obtain the moisture more efficiently, many trees, for example acacias, develop two types of roots: lateral roots close to the surface which absorb water after the rain, and a deep taproot which pumps water from the underground source. Some trees send down taproots to the water table to a depth of twenty to twenty-five meters. Many desert plants produce more biomass in their roots than in their visible aerial parts. This is why desert plants appear to grow slowly. In fact, only the aerial part is growing slowly, especially when the plant is still young: most of the energy is allocated to developing the root system. Even under irrigation, the stem growth of young desert trees is slow, especially in the first four years after planting.

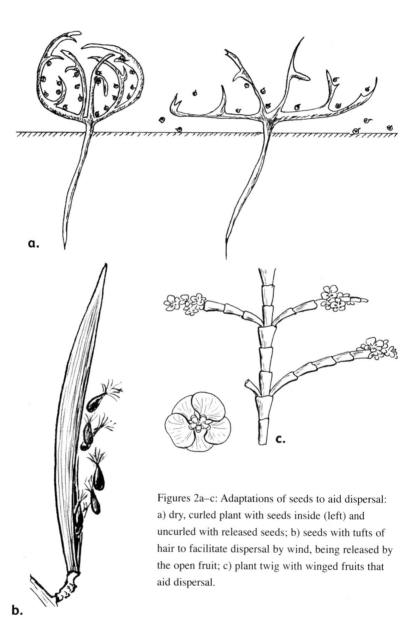

Figures 2a–c: Adaptations of seeds to aid dispersal: a) dry, curled plant with seeds inside (left) and uncurled with released seeds; b) seeds with tufts of hair to facilitate dispersal by wind, being released by the open fruit; c) plant twig with winged fruits that aid dispersal.

Other plants have extensive, but shallow roots to take advantage of each shower of rain. The distribution of the roots is the reason for the space between plants in the desert. Each plant has its own niche to obtain water.

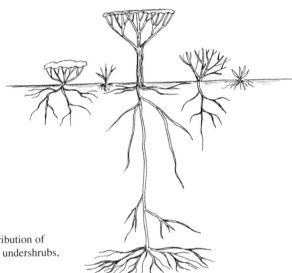

Figure 3: Root distribution of desert tree (center), undershrubs, and small plants.

To stay alive, desert plants must minimize their water loss. For this reason, they have various adaptations to conserve water and control the water movement in the plants. Because the stomata, through which up to 90 percent of the plant's moisture may be lost, are mainly present on leaf surfaces, many desert plants have small leaves while others shed leaves during the dry season. For example the rudimentary leaves of tamarisk (*Tamarix aphylla*) and white saksaul (*Haloxylon persicum*) are so small that they are difficult to see without a magnifying glass.

The desert shrubs *Capparis decidua* and *Retama raetam*, as well as the tree *Moringa peregrina*, bear small compound leaves on their young branches only in early spring, while for the rest of the year these plants stay leafless. All desert acacias have feather-like leaves which are less affected by heat than the simple large leaves and which stay on the trees in successive years, being shed only in an extremely dry period.

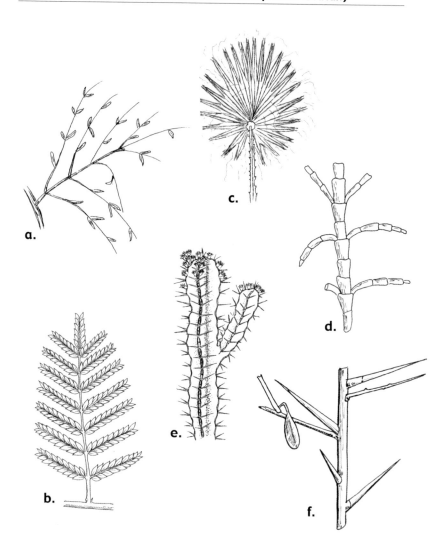

Figures 4a–f: Adaptations to water storage: a) tiny compound leaves of young branches of *Moringa peregrina*; b) feather-like acacia leaves; c) leathery palm leaf; d) succulent branch of *Anabasis*; e) succulent stem of *Euphorbia*; f) thorns of the Egyptian plum.

Leaves of other plants such as *Ficus sycomorus, Olea chrysophylla,* and the palms *Medemia argun* and *Phoenix dactylifera* are leathery, covered by wax that both protects against heat and reduces water loss. Tiny hairs on the leaves and stem of *Solenostemma* also reduce water loss by trapping water vapor near the plant surface.

Another means of survival in the desert is to store water in the plant body. Plants that do this are called succulents. Those that store water in the stem have a cactus-like appearance, a good example being some desert *Euphorbia,* such as *E. polyacantha* that grows on the slopes of the Gebel Elba Mountains. The leaves of such plants are not apparent: they have been modified into spines. Many succulents store water in their branches, including *Anabasis,* and several species of *Salsola,* while others store water in their leaves.

It is not only the harsh climate that puts great pressure on the desert plants, but also heavy grazing, against which they protect themselves by becoming thorny, developing spines and prickles. The twigs of most desert trees (acacias, Egyptian plum) are armed with sharp outgrowths of either spines or prickles. However, the young plants with less sharp spines are very vulnerable to grazing and, if cultivated, they need protection. Other plants have a repellent smell *(Salsola)* or are poisonous, such as *Calotropis* and oleander. Indeed the success of oleander as an ornamental shrub can be attributed to its poisonous compounds. It is the only plant that survives along roads in both urban and rural areas while many other plants are completely destroyed, mainly by domestic animals.

Another noticeable feature of desert vegetation is the heterogeneous distribution of plants. Topography and microhabitats play an essential role here. Even on a relatively level surface, the plant cover is denser and the plants are more vigorous in the micro-depressions compared with the slightly elevated parts. Plants take advantage of the prolonged availability of moisture, which is usually stored in the low ground.

In landscape gardening, the mosaic of microhabitats should be taken into consideration for selecting locations for the plants. The low ground will be more favorable for water-thirsty plants while the elevated parts are most suitable for those that are drought resistant. In the desert garden, care should also be given to the grouping of plants, with root distribution being the main criterion for selecting plants and their neighbors. Plants with different root lengths grow better in association. Most desert plants need direct light and will not grow in the shade of trees with compact crowns.

23

If the crown is light, as in trees with very small or feathery leaves, for example white saksaul *(Haloxylon persicum)* and *Moringa peregrina*, the filtered shade is favorable to the growth of plants under the trees.

The tree is the keystone plant in designing the garden and its position should be chosen first. Under-shrubs can be planted nearby, but not directly under the tree canopy, and shallow-rooted small perennials or annuals are placed between the shrubs and trees. For example, the following grouping of plants could be recommended: *Acacia tortilis* (tree), *Senna alexandrina* (under-shrub), *Anastatica hierochuntica* (shallow rooted annual). Another group could comprise the following: *Balanites* (tree), *Solenostemma* (under-shrub) and *Cymbopogon proximus* (shallow rooted perennial grass).

4

Types of Desert Gardens

The most popular desert garden is the ornamental and/or landscape garden which comprises desert or drought-resistant plants. A main advantage of desert plants is that they consume little water and can grow on poor soil. One purpose in growing such plants is to create a microclimate by providing shade. On a very hot summer day, the air temperature in the shade of trees can be more than ten degrees Celsius cooler than under direct sun. In addition, desert plants protect buildings from moving sand dunes by fixing sand with their roots. Such a green belt around a house or settlement combats sand and dust blown by the wind, especially during the strong *khamasin* storms which occur in spring. Moreover, some desert leguminous plants can make the garden soil more fertile by enriching it with nitrogen.

The aesthetic value of plants, such as the specific eye-catching shape of a plant or its parts (flowers, fruits, twigs, or stem) is usually taken into consideration for gardening. For example, the indigenous desert plant *hargal (Solenostemma arghel)* has gorgeous fragrant flowers; the trunk of the *doum* palm is attractively forked; the fruits of the castor oil plant are covered by an intriguing spiky outgrowth; the flattened umbrella-like crown of an acacia invites one to rest in its shade. The aesthetic value of plants is enriched by a knowledge of their ecology, history, and conservation status. To make plants more familiar to you and visitors to your garden, a good idea is to label each plant with its local and Latin names, the date of planting, and the source of the propagules (i.e., the seeds or plant parts).

If the plant is rare or threatened, you can be proud of having it in your garden, thus contributing to its conservation. For example, *argoun (Medemea argun)* and the *doum* palm are very similar in appearance to each other, except that *doum* has a more attractive branching trunk and large edible fruits. Yet the knowledge that argoun is a threatened palm in Egypt, with only a few still existing in the wild, and that you are contributing to the protection of biodiversity by sheltering this plant, would probably lead you to give it a key position in your garden; while the doum palm is better suited to planting alongside roads, in garden entrances, and around museums and archaeological sites (especially in Upper Egypt, where this plant belongs but where it has become rare because of habitat loss).

Knowledge of their uses can help in selecting plants. For example, planting the caper bush *(Capparis spinosa)* will provide you, in addition to its lovely white flowers, with delicious capers, which are the flower buds preserved in brine or vinegar.

If the garden is designed for a museum where the ancient remains of plant specimens are displayed, it is logical to select plants with a long and well-documented history. Excellent examples are the sycomore fig, *doum* and *argoun* palms, Egyptian plum, and acacias, whose remains have been found in many pharaonic tombs and are kept in museums and special collections.

Small private gardens

Garden style depends on factors such as individual taste, and the time and funds available. Your garden could be designed as a mini-oasis or private patio garden. In such gardens, native plants may contribute to the landscaping together with other common ornamental plants, which have been introduced from different areas with an arid climate.

According to the size of the garden, one or two trees with large spreading crown could be placed on the southern side of the house to provide shade and protect it from wind. In hot areas of the United States of America, it has been estimated that a mature tree with a wide canopy can cut the cooling costs of a house by 42 percent (Johnson and Harbison 1995). The native trees with large crowns that are suitable for this purpose in Egypt can be selected from the following: Nile acacia, *Acacia raddiana*, white acacia, Egyptian plum, tamarisk, Christ-thorn, and sycomore fig.[12] If your house has a simple sewage system, which is not attached to the main sewage network, the Egyptian plum will help to drain the ground by absorbing the extra moisture. The three species of palms—date, *doum*, and *argoun*—can provide a luxuriant appearance to the garden if planted in front of the house. The delicate horseradish tree *(Moringa peregrina)* with

Figure 5: Form of the *Acacia raddiana* tree growing wild in the Egyptian desert.

its long willowy and almost leafless branches will not take too much of your garden space and will allow other ornamental plants to grow under its light crown. The graceful white broom shrub will add to the appeal of your garden in spring, while the unique appearance of another leafless shrub, *arta (Calligonum polygonoides)*, with the changing shapes and colors of its flowers and fruits, will keep your attention all year round.

The real queen of the desert garden is the stunning *hargal (Solenostemma arghel)* with its lovely delicately scented white flowers which densely cover the bush in winter and attract many pollinating insects and butterflies. This small bush, pale grayish-green in appearance, remains attractive throughout the year with its fine green oval fruits, striped with dark lines and pointed ends, and velvety, spineless elongated leaves and young branches. This plant has priority for cultivation because of its outstanding ornamental value.

Figure 6: Striking *Solenostemma arghel* shrub.

The giant reed grass *(Arundo donax)*, which can reach a height of up to eight meters, symbolizes the power of arid lands to produce such colossal plants, this being one of the tallest grasses in the world.

There are many other plants which could be planted in your garden, but remember that desert plants grow slowly during the first four years, but in subsequent years they develop into huge plants which need a lot of space. When designing your garden, take this feature into consideration and space plants sufficiently to provide for their mature width and height. This will reduce competition for space and moisture, and make pruning less necessary.

Plants which are dangerous because of their poisonous compounds, such as oleander, downy thorn apple, and Sodom apple, should be avoided in the private garden, especially if you have small children who could easily poison themselves. Most desert plants have very sharp spines, which can also be hazardous if they need to be pruned.

Over-watering often creates problems. Remember that a desert plant is more likely to suffer, even die, from too much rather than from too little water.

Hotel gardens

Most four- and five-star hotels in Egypt have their own gardens, which can be very large when hotels are sited outside cities. During the last two decades, there has been intensive development of densely packed tourist resorts on the Mediterranean and Red Sea coasts. Large areas are devoted to gardens in some of these resorts, planted mainly with introduced ornamental species that are used for landscaping and are high water consumers. In the most luxurious hotels on the Red Sea coast, the diversity of ornamental plants can reach up to one hundred species. Of the native plants, only the date palm takes up its customary position in the garden, while the roads are lined with oleander, and the indigenous tamarisk tree *(Tamarix aphylla)* may be seen growing on the edges of such gardens.

These hotels and resorts are far from the river Nile, which is the main source of the water supply for all Egypt. It should be noted that Egypt already faces problems of water shortage, even in the Nile Valley. Water is pumped from the river Nile and transferred through pipes for hundreds of kilometers before it reaches the towns, villages, and tourist resorts on the seacoast. Accordingly, the cost of water there has become very expensive. Most of the larger hotels have their own sewage recycling facilities, and the treated sewage water is used for garden irrigation. However, fresh water can still be added to the irrigation system. Alkaline and saline soils on the seashores require a large amount of fresh water to wash out the salts, in order to make the land suitable for plant growth. This adds to the water consumption and hence to the water bill.

Growing indigenous desert plants with a low water intake, some of which are saline resistant or can even be salinity loving, will enrich the biodiversity of a garden, solve the salinity problem, and considerably decrease the water bill for the hotel's owners. The cost of propagules will decrease considerably, because the indigenous plants are available and

Figure 7: *Doum* palm growing along the road.

seeds or parts of plants can be collected in the wild (other than in Protected Areas) or bought in local markets. What will be needed is a small nursery for growing the plants. Most probably, many tourists staying in the hotel will be interested in the local flora, which will also attract the local fauna, particularly birds. Therefore, hotels with desert gardens will be playing a welcome role in the protection of the country's biodiversity.

There are two approaches to designing a desert garden. The first is to combine desert plants with common ornamental plants, while the second is to allocate part of the land to creating the desert garden. The date palm, *doum* palm, olive, Egyptian plum, Christ-thorn, and sycamore fig are trees which can be easily grown in combination with other ornamental plants.

Figure 8: *Acacia tortilis* growing in Eastern Desert with flat-topped crown.

However, it should be taken into consideration that native desert plants will require different irrigation regimes from other plants growing in the garden. Therefore, plants with similar water needs should be grouped, and natural land variations used to determine the groups. For example, date palms could be placed on sand dunes together with white saksaul *(Haloxylon persicum)* and *arta (Calligonum comosum)* giving the area the natural appearance of the northern coast of Sinai.

The branching *doum* palm, which is salt tolerant, can give a magnificent appearance to a hotel entrance. Trees with large spreading crowns that provide dense shade are *Acacia raddiana*, Egyptian plum, and tamarisk *(Tamarix aphylla)*, all of which can grow on slightly saline soils.

Saline gravelly ground is the most suitable habitat for *Acacia tortilis*, which grows as a shrub with a peculiar flat shaped crown in close proximity to the sea. If this acacia is planted far away from the sea, on non-saline soil, the plant grows as a large tree with the umbrella-like flat crown providing dense shade. The graceful shrubs *hargal (Solenostemma arghel)* and white broom could embellish the central area of a hotel, while the caper *(Capparis spinosa)* despite having very attractive white flowers, should be planted in places where there is no risk of visitors being hurt by their sharp spines. Sites near small lakes and pools can provide habitats for Nile acacia, *Acacia seyal*, and giant reed.

31

Most desert plants are very slow growing, so at the beginning of the garden's formation the fast growing castor oil plant and Sodom apple *(Calotropis procera)* can provide greenery and shade. However, it should be taken into consideration that Sodom apple could be dangerous because of its poisonous compounds, the same being true of the downy thorn apple *(Datura innoxia)* and oleander.

Gardens at historical sites

Special attention should be paid to gardens at historical sites, particularly archaeological sites, ancient monuments, and museums. There is a paradox between the rising interest in ancient Egyptian gardens, which are well documented, and the present day's neglected areas, with a few introduced trees, or no gardens at all, surrounding the temples which supported such magnificent gardens in the past. The situation in which the introduced Indian Laurel trees dominate most museum gardens is deplorable. The trees planted in ancient Egyptian gardens can provide the guidelines for the selection of plants for gardens around the historical sites and monuments. The following native trees were cultivated in the ancient Egyptian gardens:[13] sycomore fig *(Ficus sycomorus)*, common fig *(Ficus carica)*, date palm *(Phoenix dactylifera)*, doum palm *(Hyphaene thebaica)*, argoun *(Medemia argun)*, Egyptian plum *(Balanites aegyptiaca)*, Christ-thorn *(Ziziphus spina-christi)*, horseradish tree *(Moringa peregrina)*, olive *(Olea europaea)*, pistachio *(Pistacia sp.)*, castor oil plant *(Ricinus communis)*, and Nile acacia *(Acacia nilotica)*. These trees could form an excellent landscaped frame for Egyptian historical monuments. Many plants in these gardens, which were recorded and identified from ancient wall depictions and papyrus documents, are local desert plants that still grow wild in Egypt.

In her outstanding book *History of Garden Art*, Marie-Luise Gothein (1913) gives a fascinating description of gardens in the pharaonic period: "Every one of the forty-two districts, into which Upper and Lower Egypt were divided, had its own temple with a sacred grove attached. From very early times trees were held sacred by the Egyptians, but now each of these temples had a particular tree sacred to itself, which was chiefly, if not exclusively, cultivated in the temple garden. If we may judge by the inscriptions, the greater temples must have owned very extensive lands."

Figure 9: Plate of doum palm from *Description de l'Egypte, Histoire Naturelle*, vol. II bis, 1809. Photo IFAO, courtesy of Cultnat.

Figure 10: Plate of date palm fruits *(Phoenix dactylifera)* from *Description de l'Egypte, Histoire Naturelle*, vol. II bis, 1809. Courtesy of Cultnat.

Figure 11: Wall painting of *doum* and date palms, tomb of Sennedjem, Deir el-Medina. Courtesy of Cultnat.

In designing the garden the outstanding historical value of the sycomore fig should be stressed as reflected in the description by Gothein (1913): "It is very often mentioned, and in the old records the hieroglyph for Sycomore often stands for Tree in general. It seems that, according to a very ancient belief, a Sycomore stood under the canopy of heaven beside both the rising and the setting of the sun; it was supposed to be of malachite, perhaps to indicate its imperishable green hue. The fruit and the wood of this tree are both of use; in its shade the living rejoice as well as the dead, and the peasant honors it as especially sacred, and sacrifices to it the fruits of the earth."

An invaluable record of the trees in an Eighteenth Dynasty garden has been bequeathed to us by Ineni, a Theban building supervisor who built a house for himself, "whose main attraction was a magnificent garden." The house and the garden behind is depicted in Ineni's tomb (no. 81 at Thebes) and a complete inventory of the trees he planted in his orchard was included: "73 sycamore trees; 31 persea trees; 170 date-palms; 120 *dom*-palms; 5 fig trees; 2 moringa trees; 12 vines; 5 pomegranate trees; 16 carob trees; 5 Christ thorn; 1 *argun*-palm; 8 willow trees; 10 tamarisk trees . . ." (Manniche 1999).

Figure 12: Plate of sycomore fig tree from Frederic Louis Norden's *Voyage d'Egypte et de Nubie*, after Marcus Tuscher, Copenhagen, 1755. Courtesy of Cultnat.

In addition to the plants mentioned above, the native acacias are perfect candidates for the temple gardens. *Acacia tortilis* subsp. *tortilis* (Umbrella thorn), *Acacia tortilis* subsp. *raddiana*, and *Acacia ehrenbergiana*, which are drought resistant, are suitable for desert historical sites. Other native water-loving acacias, *Acacia laeta* and *Acacia seyal* could be planted in the temple garden close to a lake or pool. Both acacias are rare in Egypt and their planting would contribute to the protection of biodiversity. The outstanding ability of the apple ring acacia *(Faidherbia albida)* to grow in periodically inundated areas and withstand long inundation periods make this tree the most appropriate for planting on the shores and islands of Lake Nasser (Aswan High Dam Lake) where the ancient monuments of Nubia were relocated.

To make a place green and attractive in a short time, fast growing plants, such as the castor oil plant and the Sodom apple may be planted. These two plants will grow up to three meters high and produce fruits in two years. The annual plants rose of Jericho *(Anastatica hierochuntica)* and the downy thorn apple *(Datura innoxia)* will give a striking appearance in a few months. The latter species, which is already popular throughout the world as a decorative plant, can grow up to one meter high. It produces substantial foliage and glorious large funnel-like flowers in the spring. The rose of Jericho spreads over the ground in the spring and curls up into a ball when dry in the summer.

35

Plants in the new desert settlements and alongside roads and streets

Urbanization in Egypt, as in most countries all over the world, has speeded up in the recent period. The desert land surrounding large Egyptian cities, particularly Cairo, has been developed to build satellite towns, which provide industrial centers and modest housing for the fast growing Egyptian population. Because of the high solar radiation in these new desert settlements, their greening is an essential issue; yet water shortage and the high cost of irrigation are major constraints in developing green areas. Even when underground water is pumped out, the cost remains high because of energy consumption. Thus the cultivation of the desert plants with low water requirements could contribute to water conservation and decrease the cost of irrigation. Trees with large crowns providing dense shade, such as the acacias *A. raddiana* and *A. pachyceras*, the apple ring acacia (*Faidherbia albida*), the Egyptian plum, tamarisk, Christ-thorn, and sycomore fig are most useful decorative and shade trees for gardens and streets. Tamarisk and Egyptian plum can be sheared into a dense hedge, excellent for use as a screen against wind, dust, and blown sand. They also serve to stabilize the sand where they grow.

Alleys of *doum* and date palms, together with colorful oleander shrubs and *hargal* on the ground will give a magnificent appearance to public gardens. It is important to note that both oleander and *hargal* have a disagreeable taste, the former being actually poisonous to animals, so that if Bedouins from the surrounding desert bring their livestock of goats and sheep to browse, they will never eat either of these two plants. The tamarisk, Christ-thorn, olive, and oleander are among the most suitable plants for growing along roads and highways. The last two already grow along the Cairo-Alexandria Desert Highway.

5

Gardens for Education and Research

Gardens with indigenous plants could provide excellent facilities in schools, universities, and other institutions, for teaching and learning, in the field, the different natural science subjects such as environmental science, botany, and ecology. At the same time they can increase awareness about the protection of local flora.

School gardens

In most Egyptian schools, space for a garden is very limited and plants need to be selected carefully. These plants should have ornamental value, to be attractive at different seasons, and they should provide shade. Those with an interesting background and history should have priority, so that stories about them will attract the children's attention. In addition, they must be safe, non-poisonous and without spines that could injure children who touch them. Of the plants described in this book, the most appropriate for planting in the school ground are sycomore fig *(Ficus sycomorus)* and tamarisk *(Tamarix aphylla)*, both of which are evergreen trees without spines, whose large spreading crowns provide good shade. The sycomore fig is an excellent example of a tree that can be studied in history, art, biology,[14] ecology, and conservation. The history of the sycomore fig is well known and has been mentioned above in this book. In the pharaonic period, its symbol was used as a hieroglyph for all trees. In the more recent past, it was a tree much loved among Egyptian peasants. A poem about it is cited in Marie-Luise Gothein's *History of Garden Art*:[15]

The little sycamore,
Which she planted with her own hand,
She moves her lips to speak.
How fair are her lovely branches!
She is laden with fruits
That are redder than the jasper.

Both sycamore and tamarisk are long lived but slow growing trees. To make the school garden green, the fast growing *saisaban (Sesbania sesban)* and castor oil plant can be planted. Other suitable plants for the school garden that do not take much space are *doum (Hyphaene thebaica)* and date palms *(Phoenix dactylifera)*.

Figure 13: Old sycamore fig tree growing beside the road leading to the Aswan Dam.

University gardens

Gardens at universities have to be designed to fulfill the complementary functions of education and research. The desert garden in a university campus could be considered as an outdoor laboratory for the practical classes in teaching the different aspects of biology, such as ecology, pharmacology, botany, and zoology. In the warm climate of Egypt, such a garden will fulfill its function throughout the academic year.

In the last three decades, there has been a tendency to build universities outside towns and cities to provide space for the university campus and its future development. If the space allows, an area should be allocated for a desert garden, which should be established without disturbing the natural features. A small greenhouse or plant nursery could be an important component of such a garden.

Diversity of plant species, representing different families with distinct morphological and physiological characteristics, and consideration of plant uses, such as in traditional medicine, as food, fodder for animals, and fuel, should influence the selection of plants for education and research purposes.[16]

Figure 14: *Halfa barr (Cymbopogon proximus)* planted in experimental farm in Wadi Allaqi.

Almost every university could afford its own teaching garden, while the garden's design would depend on local conditions. Success will depend on the contributions of specialists from different disciplines (mainly biology, agriculture, and pharmacology) in designing and establishing such a garden. Each plant described in this book could have its role in such a garden.

University gardens provide an excellent facility for research work. There are endless lists of research topics related to desert plants. Experiments conducted on the reproduction of indigenous plants could help in establishing and enriching the species diversity of the garden and promoting the establishment of new gardens. Research on the water requirements of the desert plants would facilitate the maintenance of the garden by providing useful information on the necessary water supply. Field experiments could be designed to investigate the remarkable ability of some indigenous plants, such as white acacia *(Faidherbia albida)* and tamarisk to tolerate long drought periods and survive prolonged inundation.

In studying the medicinal use of plants a large amount of plant material is usually needed, which is almost impossible to obtain in the wild: some plants grow only in Protected Areas and others are very rare, for example *argoun (Medemia* palm) and *halfa barr (Cymbopogon proximus).* In addition, most desert plants grow only after rain, which is very scarce and unpredictable, especially in southern Egypt. Accordingly, many years might pass before the material required could be tracked down. Plants cultivated in the desert garden would provide the material needed for research.

The desert garden at the Aswan campus of South Valley University

An interesting and attractive example of a multi-purpose desert garden has been created at the Aswan campus of South Valley University. The Aswan campus is located on the shores of the reservoir between the High Dam and Aswan Dam, where an extensive area of virgin desert was allocated for its establishment in the 1980s. It had heterogeneous topographic features and diversity of habitats, as well as only a limited development area for the construction of buildings (less than 20 percent of the total university land area). This provided ideal conditions for creating a desert garden.

The garden's history began in 1997, when a few rare and threatened desert species were planted on the university campus, namely Egyptian plum *(Balanites aegyptiaca)*, castor oil plant *Ricinus communis* (the desert variety), *halfa barr (Cymbopogon proximus)* and *hargal (Solenostemma arghel)*. Seeds and seedlings of these plants were collected from remote areas in the southern part of the Eastern Desert. The initial purpose was to reproduce these rare desert plants in order to secure a stock. Apart from *Cymbopogon proximus*, all the plants were grown from seeds, which were first germinated in pots and then planted out in the garden.

A few young individuals of *halfa barr* came from the Egat area on the border with Sudan, where the small population of this grass still grows in Egypt. It is widely sold in markets throughout Egypt because of its high medicinal value, and is also a common refreshing drink ordered in coffee shops and local restaurants, especially in Upper Egypt. It was difficult to grow from seed: the seeds only germinated when the tissue culture method was applied. However, several years later the grass started to grow from the seeds spread by the mother plants, which regenerated naturally in the desert garden wherever they found a suitable habitat with moist soil. The most favorable habitats have proved to be rocky places and tree-bases, where seeds have collected and formed a seed bank. At least a one-year period of dormancy in the ground is required before seeds germinate, but once the plants are established, they grow naturally. This also applies to *Solenostemma arghel*, another threatened desert plant, which is widely used in traditional medicine and commonly sold in the markets.

In 1998, one year after founding the garden, we decided to extend it in order to conserve indigenous acacia trees. We started with acacias characteristic of the Nile Valley, whose seeds were collected on the First Cataract Islands in Aswan. Seedlings of *Acacia arabica*, *Acacia nilotica*, and *Acacia seyal* were planted on an almost flat area covered by a dense sheet of sand, while *Acacia laeta* and *Faidherbia albida* were planted on slightly elevated rocky ground where pockets of sand had accumulated between the rocks. The most successful were *A. seyal*, *A. laeta* and *Faidherbia albida*, which grew very fast and reached maturity in approximately three years when they began to produce seeds. The growth of *A. nilotica* and *A. arabica* was slower than that of the other acacias and they were threatened through competition, mainly with *A. seyal*. Only one *A. arabica* tree succeeded in growing but feebly and did not mature. *A. arabica* is a plant threatened with extinction throughout Egypt.

41

In the next few years, the acacia garden was extended with the planting of typical desert acacias, namely *Acacia tortilis* subsp. *raddiana, Acacia tortilis* subsp. *tortilis* and *Acacia ehrenbergiana,* which grow in the surrounding desert. All these trees are very slow growing compared with the Nile Valley acacias. Recently, from 2003 to 2004, we tried to plant *Acacia pachyceras* (syn. *A. gerrardii*) seedlings in this desert garden but without as much success as the other acacias, which are native to the southern part of Egypt.

Part of the garden is available for the cultivation of threatened indigenous palms: the *doum* palm *(Hyphaene thebaica)* and *argoun* palm *(Medemia argun).* These two palms are native to Egypt and in particular to Upper Egypt. The *doum* palm grows naturally along the banks of the Nile in Upper Egypt, as well as being cultivated in gardens. A few individuals even grow as far north as Cairo, for example in the Orman Garden in Giza.

About 40 *doum* palms and 30 *argoun* palms are now growing in the desert garden. Because the *doum* palms were planted a few years earlier than the *argoun* palms, some individuals already have a well-defined trunk and have begun fruiting, while the *argoun* palms, which are only two to three years old, are still very small. Because this is the first attempt at cultivating *argoun,* there is no information available on its growth rate, but it seems that this palm is similar to the *doum* in that it too is slow growing.

Other trees planted in the garden are *Tamarix aphylla* and *Ziziphus spina-christi,* the former propagated from cuttings and the latter from seed.

Sprinkler irrigation is used in most parts of the garden: water is applied in the form of a spray, reaching the soil very much as rain does. Because all of the garden area receives water, the seeds of many desert plants which were lying dormant in the soil or had been brought there by wind or in other ways, such as by birds or mammals, have begun to germinate and by 2005 more than 30 desert plants have established themselves in this garden. Surprisingly, there are almost no weeds among them, perhaps because neither silt soil from the Nile Valley nor any kind of fertilizer has been used.

These self-germinating plants include many well known for their medicinal properties, for example *Senna alexandrina, Pulicaria incisa, Datura innoxia* and *Hyoscyamus muticus.* Not only herbs, but also shrubs such as *Calotropis procera, Sesbania sesban* and *Tamarix nilotica* are growing naturally in this garden.

The green vegetation and water have attracted predators. Many reptiles have appeared in this garden including numerous lizards, and some dangerous species, such as the viper and even the cobra, have been seen there. The garden has become a home for the desert hare and for small rodents; the Rüppell's Sand Fox is a common visitor to the garden to feed on the rodents. Resident birds live in the garden and migratory species visit during the periods of migration. On flowering *Acacia seyal* and *Ziziphus spina-christi* trees, Nile Valley Sunbirds (both male and female) have been seen in springtime and the acacias have attracted numerous Red-vented Bulbuls and Common Bulbuls.

It is a truly multipurpose garden, which at present has the following functions: plant conservation, a demonstration desert garden, education (student field-classes), and research.

Halfa barr plant surrounded by acacias in the desert garden at the Aswan campus of South Valley University.

6
Collection and Propagation of Desert Plants

D esert plants are propagated in different ways from other ornamental plants. Most ornamental plants used for gardening and urban planning originated in various parts of the world and need special care to grow successfully when introduced to areas with alien climates. In *The Street Trees of Egypt* by el-Hadidi and Boulos (1989) of a total fifty-seven ornamental plants growing in the streets of Egyptian towns and cities, only seven are listed as indigenous to Egypt. There is a similar situation in the arid countries of North Africa and the Middle East, where introduced plants are mainly used for ornamental purposes.

The most common practice is propagating and growing plants in nurseries or greenhouses under the care of specialists until they reach an age suitable for replanting. Saplings of date palm, oleander, and olive are commonly sold in plant nurseries. Yet in spite of the many plant nurseries burgeoning in Egypt, only a limited number of indigenous plants, such as Nile acacia, tamarisk, Christ-thorn and sycomore fig, are available for sale in a few nurseries. Outstandingly rich in indigenous plants is the nursery of Dina Aly's garden in the Oraby district near Cairo, where she propagates many desert plants.[17] On the Botanical Island in Aswan a small number of *doum* palms are propagated and sold to the public.

Under such circumstances, those who would like to create a desert garden and grow indigenous plants will have to depend on their own experience and experimentation in plant propagation. Difficulties facing such enthusiasts include insufficient or inaccessible information on this subject in Egypt. Among the most reliable sources is Kees Vogt's *A Field Worker's Guide* (1995) on the propagation of trees in Sudan, where some of the plants described are similar to those in Egypt.

Availability of propagules

Plants are propagated by means of sexual reproduction (seeds) and/or asexual (vegetative) reproduction (parts of the plant). The propagation materials (whether seeds or parts of plants) are termed propagules.

The first question is where and how to obtain the material for propagation of indigenous plants. Access to plant material is not easy; collection of seeds or parts of plants in the wild can damage the natural population of the plants; some plants are rare, growing only in Protected Areas; a few grow in remote areas that are difficult to reach.

If you are not able to travel to these desert areas, careful observation may help you to collect the propagules from your surroundings. Some indigenous plants (Christ-thorn tree, acacias, tamarisk) grow in urban and rural neighborhoods, at the sides of roads and in public gardens in Upper Egypt, as well as in the Orman Botanical Garden in Giza and the Agricultural Museum garden in Doqqi. Huge sycomore figs grow in old downtown Cairo gardens and on the Nile Corniche. There are at least five indigenous tree species in the Maadi district including the Nile acacia, sycomore fig, *doum* palm, castor oil tree and tamarisk (Soliman and Amer 2002).

A short journey to the New Cairo district will give you the chance to encounter and observe some fascinating desert plants, which you might well like to have in your garden. On the new campus of the American University in Cairo, as well as in the surrounding desert, white broom *(Retama raetam)*, an elegant legume shrub, flowers abundantly in spring and fruits in summer. In springtime, you can see here the rose of Jericho *(Anastatica hierochuntica)* the amazing annual, which lies almost prostrate on the ground while green, but in summer when the seeds mature, it sheds its green leaves and curls up its woody fruiting branches to form a globular body, waiting for the next rain to open it and disperse the seeds. Unfortunately, this plant has become rare in the Egyptian desert especially near large towns, most probably because of over-collecting for sale in plant shops. The striking fruits of *arta (Calligonum polygonoides)* will catch your eye as you pass; they are red when young, and covered by soft yellow hairs when mature.

Upper Egypt is especially rich in plant material for propagation. Seeds of some acacias can be collected from the trees growing on the Nile banks. The seeds of the Christ-thorn tree are sold in the local market in Assiut, where this tree grows abundantly in the surrounding area. The town of Aswan is the only place in Egypt where the huge *Acacia laeta* trees are still growing in gardens (one example is the Cataract Hotel garden) and on Elephantine (Aswan) Island. The Botanical Island (formerly known as Kitchener's Island) gives refuge to a few indigenous acacias, *doum* palms, and the toothbrush tree *(Salvadora persica)*.

Remains of the natural vegetation still exist on the First Cataract Islands. Two of these islands (Saluga and Ghazel) are Protected Areas, where seeds of acacias (*Acacia nilotica, A. seyal, A. laeta, Faidherbia albida*, and *A. raddiana*) can be obtained with prior permission from the Egyptian Environmental Affairs Agency (EEAA) in Cairo[18] or its branch in Aswan. The rangers of these conservation islands are very cooperative and can provide useful information on when, where, and how to collect the seeds.

It is also possible to visit the desert garden at the Aswan campus of South Valley University, which is situated between Aswan Dam and Aswan High Dam on the road to the airport. A description of the garden has been given in this book. The staff of the Unit of Environmental Studies and Development, the institution within the University[19] responsible for this garden, are very helpful to visitors, who will be given practical guidelines on cultivation of the desert plants growing there. It may also be possible to get hold of propagules (seeds and parts) of some plants. Usually available are *halfa barr* grass, seeds of *hargal (Solenostemma arghel)*, acacias (*A. laeta* and *A. seyal*), *Faidherbia albida* and Egyptian plum *(Balanites aegyptiaca)*. Seeds of the *argoun* palm *(Medemia argun)* are limited in number because it is a very rare plant: only two fruiting individuals remain in Egypt. However, the seeds could be obtained from Sudan where this palm still grows, though not as abundantly as in the past.

Other sources of seeds are local markets and specialized shops selling plants used in traditional medicine and customs. The main suppliers of indigenous medicinal plants are the Bedouins who collect these throughout Egypt. These places are good sources of seeds including the *doum* palm, horseradish tree *(Moringa peregrina)* and Egyptian plum, all of which are sold for their edible fruits and their medicinal value. The seeds of the rose of Jericho (*Anastatica hierochuntica*) are found inside the dry plants on sale in the markets.

Access to the Internet has become easy and inexpensive throughout Egypt. Seeds of some plants may be purchased through numerous Internet websites. These include white saksaul, *(Haloxylon persicum)*, downy thorn apple *(Datura innoxia)*, *Capparis decidua*, caper *(Capparis spinosa)*,

Calligonum polygonoides, and senna *(Senna alexandrina)*. Internet references to some plants are given in Chapter 8: Plant Descriptions.

However, there are still many plants that can only be collected in the wild. The best way to proceed is to contact the EEAA, Sector of Nature Protection, and ask for advice. This authority is responsible for nature conservation, particularly for the protection of biodiversity to assure that wildlife will not decline as result of overexploitation. Another source is personal communication with people working on desert plants who can help with seed collection as well as advice on seed germination.[20]

Storing seeds

When seeds are collected, they should be appropriately stored to ensure that they will not be infected by fungus or eaten by insects, and that the seed's embryo will stay alive. It is very important to have an adequate stock of seeds, especially when there are difficulties in obtaining seeds from the wild.

Storage conditions depend on the nature of seeds, particularly the seed coat, and the prevailing climate. The best conditions for storing seeds are dry, cool, dark places. Fortunately in Egypt, with its predominantly dry climate, seeds can be stored just at normal room temperature (open storage), and most desert seeds have hard seed coats that protect the embryos.

The seeds of some plants, which are susceptible to insects, including most legume species, particularly acacias, should be fumigated or be treated with a suitable insecticide prior to storage. Powder insecticide is better than aerosol since the spray will destroy the living insects but not their eggs. Good protection from insects[21] is achieved by applying naphthalene, a simple and effective chemical compound widely sold in shops and pharmacies as a moth repellent.

In areas with high air humidity such as the sea coast, and even in Cairo, where humidity is raised at certain times of the year, the storage of dry seeds in sealed containers is recommended. Seeds can be stored for a long time without damage in well-sealed tins, aluminum cans, or glass jars, which are completely resistant to moisture transmission. Be sure to label and date them. Polythene bags also are effective: pack the seeds in two layers of polythene bags, with the dated identification label inserted between the inner and outer one, so that plant names will be visible. Treated seeds in well-sealed containers can be stored for up to five years without loss of viability.

Pre-sowing treatment of seeds

Seeds of most desert plants need a resting period after maturity, before they can germinate; this is known as the dormancy period. Some seeds develop special chemical substances that inhibit the seed germination (growth inhibitors), while others have a hard coat that prevents penetration of water and the growth of the embryo.

There are different methods of treating seeds to break dormancy. For seeds with hard coats, the best known is chemical treatment with sulfuric acid (this corrosive acid should always be used with maximum care) and mechanical treatment by abrasion of the hard seed coat, after the seeds have been soaked in either warm or cold water for a short period. Some other seeds only need to be soaked or well washed with water to flush out the growth inhibitors and/or soften the seed coat to let water penetrate inside the seed. The period of soaking in water varies from a few hours, for example in *Solenostemma arghel*, to almost a month for the *doum* palm.

Some seeds do not respond to any treatment to enhance germination. Such seeds, for example *halfa barr*, need to stay in the soil for more than one year before seeds will germinate. Other seeds do not have a dormancy period and will germinate as soon as sufficient water is available, for example the rose of Jericho and Sodom apple. In Chapter 8 on plant description, the treatment of seeds will be given for each particular plant.

Seed germination

A ripe seed consists of the embryo and stored food supply, which is enclosed in a protective cover or seed coat. To develop into a new plant, the seed needs special conditions for the embryo to begin to grow. Essential conditions for seed germination are water, a suitable temperature, and oxygen. For some seeds, light is essential while others germinate in the dark or are light neutral.

These are a few methods of germinating seeds. Small seeds can be germinated in Petri-dishes on wet filter paper placed on the bottom of the dish. (Use distilled water and do not completely cover the seeds, because embryo growth needs oxygen.) The Petri-dish is then covered to prevent growth of fungi and evaporation of water. When the radicle (primary root) protrudes though the seed coat and the plumule (primary shoot) emerges, the seedlings can be transplanted into pots.

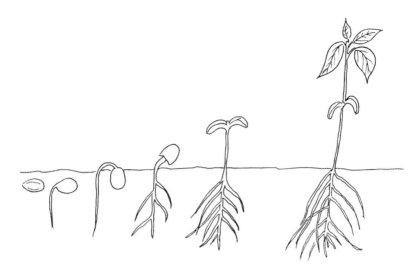

Figure 15: Stages of seed germination, showing from left to right: the seed; the embryonic root as it protrudes and then elongates; the rudimentary shoot emerges with two cotyledon leaves; and, finally the seedling develops.

Seeds also can be sown directly into pots filled with soil to which ordinary water is added. Depending on the seed, germination can take from one day (rose of Jericho) to about two or three months (*doum* palm). Seeds are commonly sown directly into the ground to propagate a large number of plants. In the former Soviet Union, the seeds of white saksaul were spread by the use of airplanes in the arid southern part of country (the Garagum and Qyzylqum deserts).

Vegetative propagation

Vegetative, or asexual propagation, is reproduction by parts of plants: stem, roots, and leaves. The new plant produced in this way is identical with the mother plant. Many herbaceous plants reproduce vegetatively by specialized underground organs, such as rhizomes, runnels, bulbs, and corms. Some desert trees, including Egyptian plum, white acacia, and the date palm, produce suckers. Suckers are shoots growing from the lower part of the trunk or stem and the root, which are able to develop their own roots and grow into new plants.

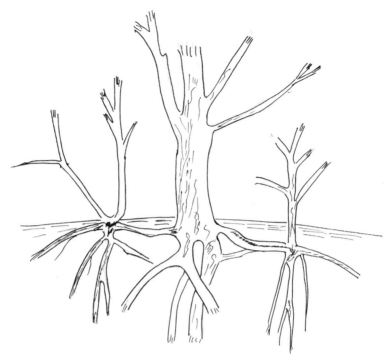

Figure 16: Suckers (shoots growing from the roots) of apple ring acacia.

The ability of plants to reproduce vegetatively was noted long ago and this method of plant reproduction is widely used in agriculture. There are many advantages of vegetative reproduction, especially for plants whose seeds do not easily germinate, such as those with tiny seeds or seeds requiring a long dormancy period. Obtaining the propagules for vegetative propagation is much easier than collecting seeds which ripen in certain seasons, mainly during the hottest months of the year (a factor that adds to the difficulty of making collecting trips especially in remote desert areas).

Nowadays, almost all plants can be vegetatively propagated by using sophisticated micro-propagation techniques or tissue culture. However, in some species, known as easy-to-root woody plants, it is simple to grow new plants because they have the ability to develop adventitious roots[22] from the woody parts of the stem. Such plants proliferate when the stem-cutting method is used.

Because not all plants described in this book are easy to propagate vegetatively, some being difficult-to-root, the recommendation for the most effective propagation method is given for each particular plant in Chapter 8. Some desert trees and shrubs described in this book could be propagated by so-called 'hardwood cuttings,'[23] a method that does not require special equipment or experience.

Usually in Egypt, most work in gardens and orchards begins in *amshir*, a month whose name comes from the Coptic calendar though it was already identified in the pharaonic calendar as the best time for planting, being at the end of winter/beginning of spring (February–March). The most successful cuttings can be taken at this time as well.

The best stock for cuttings is branches from two to three years old, selected from trees or shrubs that are healthy and moderately vigorous. Shoots that bear only leaves are better for cuttings than shoots with flowers. Cuttings should be about 15–20 cm in length; the best results are observed in cuttings taken from the basal or central portion of the shoot. In preparing the cuttings, it is often recommended to retain a small slice of old wood (known as the heel) at the base of the cutting for the best rooting result. The basal part of the cutting should be taken just below the node and its top 1–1.5 cm above the node. In non-heel cutting or straight cutting, it is important to take cuttings that are angled at the basal part and flat on the top. The slanting end should be put into the ground. Such a cut facilitates the uptake of water and nutrients from the soil. There should be at least a few buds, which are auxin producers, on the cuttings to stimulate the formation of adventitious roots (Hartmann *et al.* 1990).

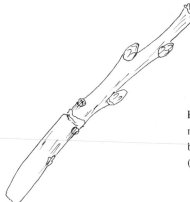

Figure 17: Part of a young twig with terminal and lateral buds, nodes (where the bud is attached to the stem) and internodes (the part of the stem between two nodes).

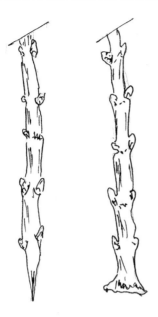

Figure 18: Types of hardwood cuttings: straight cutting with pointed end (left) and heel cutting with a small piece of wood remaining at the base (right).

The best time of the day to collect cuttings is early morning when cuttings are still turgid (not wilting). If cuttings cannot be planted immediately, they should be wrapped in a wet cloth and stored in a cool place to prevent desiccation. If properly stored, cuttings can be kept for a few days. If you wish to transport them, put them in a thick dark plastic bag in the shadiest and coolest part of the vehicle.

To facilitate formation of roots on 'difficult-to-root' cuttings, substances known as growth regulators are used. Plant growth regulators are either synthetic compounds or plant hormones that regulate the growth of plants. Some of these regulators influence the initiation of roots. Auxins, in particular, are highly effective in the formation of adventitious roots in stem cuttings. Both natural auxin compounds, such as Indole-3-acetic acid (IAA), and synthetic ones, such as indolebutyric acid (IBA) and naphthaleneacetic acid (NAA), are widely used. Growth regulators are applied to the cuttings prior to their being inserted into rooting media. All these compounds IAA, IBA, and NAA can be purchased from specialized agricultural stores in Egypt; their respective instructions for application should be strictly observed.

Containers and soil used

Containerization has many advantages compared with direct sowing of seeds and planting of cuttings into the ground. The surrounding conditions can be controlled to optimize seedling growth, especially important in hot, arid climates where temperature monitoring and the watering of seedlings should be on a daily basis. Seedlings grown in containers suffer little transplant shock when planted out, because root disturbance is minimized. Containerization also increases the period during which seedlings may be planted out, compared with the more limited period during which seedlings sown directly in the ground may be transplanted to another site.

Many kinds of containers for propagation and for growing plants in nurseries are available on the market. Not all of them are suitable for desert plants. It should be noted that desert plants develop extensive root systems, which are several times larger than their aerial parts. This is especially true at the beginning of plant growth. Some plants develop a taproot that can reach a length of up to one meter before the shoot will be seen, as in the palm, for example. The containers selected should encourage the development of strong and extensive root systems and be robust enough to enable a seedling to grow in them for up to one year without its roots protruding. The seedlings of woody desert plants should be grown in deep containers whose depth is at least twice their width.

A variety of containers is available in specialized agricultural shops: plastic bags, plastic pots, and clay pots. The cheapest is the plastic bag, which is also very light and easy to carry. Good quality plastic bags can be used for almost one year without splitting. Apart from palms, most desert plants can be propagated by using plastic bags. Holes for water drainage must be made at the bottom of the bag. Dark plastic bags absorb the heat, so the soil temperature in them increases considerably. On very hot summer days, the surface temperature may reach 70°C. High temperatures will negatively affect the growth of seedlings by slowing the development of roots, reducing water absorption, and increasing water evaporation from the soil surface. To reduce the heat, light-colored plastic bags are recommended for use in hot climates.

The plastic pots available on the market are of different sizes and qualities. Plants can stay in such containers for a longer period than in plastic bags, and are easy to transport because the pots are both light and strong. However, if plants are kept too long in such containers, the roots can protrude through the large opening at the base.

Another type of container available on the Egyptian market is the clay pot, which is very useful for growing seedlings of desert plants. The great advantage of such pots is that their walls are porous, thus increasing soil aeration and cooling the soil by allowing water to evaporate. Seedlings can stay a long time in the pots (more than one year), permitting vigorous root growth to develop. After the seedlings are planted out, the pots can be reused. However, there are some disadvantages. The pots can be easily broken; their weight can create difficulties when transporting the seedlings from the nursery to the garden. Their higher cost, compared with that of plastic bags, should also be taken into consideration. Clay pots can be recommended for the propagation of plants with extremely intensive roots, such as *doum* and *argoun* palms, and acacia trees.

For most plants, the best substratum for germination of seeds and growth of seedlings is a mixture of two parts sand to one part silt. Some plants grow better in more sandy soil, for example *Acacia ehrenbergiana,* while *Acacia nilotica* thrives in heavier soil. Cuttings of tamarisk *(Tamarix aphylla)* produce more vigorous roots in light sandy soil than in heavy soil. Recommendations on type of soil are given in the plant descriptions in Chapter 8.

For planting out from pots to the ground, the best time is early spring, February through March. Plants also grow well in Egypt when they are planted out in late fall (November).

Protection of seedlings

Newly planted seedlings are very sensitive to the harsh conditions of the desert. Particularly in spring time, the hot waves of strong, dust-laden southerly winds, the *khamasin*, blowing from the Sahara across Egypt and over the Red Sea, can destroy weak plants, erode the soil, and bury seedlings and young plants in sand. Winds can harmfully affect the water balance of plants by loss of water through evapotranspiration, leading to the plants drying out. The best protection from wind is to establish a windbreak on the southern side of each line of seedlings or to surround each young plant with a shelter, often made from matting or a wooden frame.

The soft, tender, and luscious seedlings attract domestic livestock and predators from the surrounding desert, among which desert hares, rodents, and even foxes are the most common visitors to the desert garden. Birds are attracted to freshly seeded flowerbeds. Bird netting for seedling protection is easy to use in small areas. Another method is to spread a mulch of dried leaves or shredded palm fronds over the bed. When using mulch, check every few days for emerging seedlings and be sure to remove the mulch as soon as the seedlings appear.

7

Irrigation Techniques

Various irrigation systems are used in dry lands for crop production, not all of which can be recommended for naturalistic or landscaped desert gardens. The type of irrigation selected for a desert garden depends on many factors, of which the most important is the purpose of establishing such a garden. For example its aim might be to provide students with plant material for study and to act as a site for field work. This desert garden would need a different irrigation system than a garden located near historical monuments or archaeological sites. In the first case, sprinkler irrigation could be used, in which water is applied in the form of a spray and reaches the soil very much as rain does. It irrigates large areas of the surface and encourages the spontaneous growth of desert plants from seed banks found in the garden area. In the second case, localized irrigation such as drip or subsurface irrigation should be applied, which brings water directly to the roots of planted species, hence avoiding the invasion of unwanted plants.

Other factors to be taken into consideration include water availability, the ecology of the plants selected, soil properties, funds available (irrigation costs), the size of the garden, its location, whether urban or rural, and the distance from sources of water. Of these factors water availability is critical for drylands.

Flood or surface irrigation is the traditional irrigation system in the Nile Valley, which has been used with some modification from pharaonic times until today. In spite of its wide use in farmland for crop production, this form of irrigation cannot be recommended for landscape gardening in desert lands situated outside the Nile Valley. Even in the Nile Valley the digging of canals, which is an essential requirement for such irrigation, would modify the landscape, transforming it into flattened farmlands and reducing its aesthetic value.

Following are descriptions of types of irrigation techniques which could be applied in a desert garden.

Drip or trickle irrigation systems

The sprinkler system (a device that sends a revolving spray of water onto a garden or lawn) is more efficient than flood irrigation but even this is not sufficient for such an extremely arid area as Egypt. It can be recommended only for certain purposes, such as to stimulate the germination of dormant seeds in a seed bank and for self-propagation of garden plants.

A more effective method is the drip or trickle irrigation system which is often used for desert reclamation. Trickle irrigation is defined as a frequent slow application of water to soil through emitters located at selected points, often at each plant, along water delivery pipelines. The advantage of this system is that it uses a small quantity of water, which is easy to control and can be applied at a suitable time for irrigation in the evening and at night. This system facilitates weed control and restricts the self-reproduction of plants from seeds, because it is applied only to a limited area at the base of each plant, leaving the rest of the land dry.

Drip irrigation is successfully used for the reclamation of large desert areas. However, the area of the desert garden is usually small, and if it is surrounded by desert, drip irrigation may well produce surprising and unpredictable consequences. Despite its advantage in using only about half the water consumed by other current forms of irrigation, drip irrigation is expensive to install, the water source needs to be filtered to prevent the emitters from clogging, and careful maintenance by qualified specialists is required. It can also create problems by increasing the salinity of a heavy soil (with a large amount of silt) and encouraging the development of a surface-root system that injures plant growth, especially in trees and shrubs.

In drip irrigation, the running water in the tubes imitates water running in roots, and this attracts animals. The desert hare in particular can destroy an entire irrigation system, severing small tubes by biting them to obtain water while small shoots and branches of cultivated plants provide an excellent fodder. However, by eating the vegetative branches, animals such as the desert hare effect a natural pruning of desert trees that helps them to withstand drought by decreasing the water lost through transpiration and at the same time stimulating the development of a deep root system.

Considering these factors, drip irrigation could be recommended for irrigating plants with shallow roots, but otherwise, has a limited application in a desert garden.[24]

Subsurface irrigation

To create a desert garden with indigenous desert plants a simple and low-cost subsurface irrigation system is recommended. The main principle of this irrigation is to control the water delivery by bringing water directly to roots; the water will be absorbed by the roots more efficiently without being lost by soil percolation and, most importantly, by evaporation from soil surface. Other important advantages of subsurface irrigation are that it does not increase soil salinity, it can be used without pressured and filtered water, and is unlikely to be damaged by animals and insects. Because the water is added below the soil surface, it prevents the growth of weeds, the seeds of which are abundantly present in the soil.

A traditional technique such as pitcher (buried clay pot) irrigation is best suited for cultivation of plants that are not deeply rooted. For desert trees, the most effective is the tube subsurface irrigation, which has been tested in Wadi Allaqi Biosphere Reserve field station in the south of the Eastern Desert.

Buried clay pot irrigation

The pitcher or buried clay pot irrigation is the traditional system used in dry lands for the irrigation of small farms and gardens; it is more efficient than drip irrigation and up to ten times more efficient in water conservation than surface irrigation.[25] The buried pot provides water to the roots of plants that are planted close to it. Pots are filled with water and the water seeps out through the clay wall of the buried clay pot at a rate that is influenced by the plant's own water consumption.

In Egypt, the manufacture of clay and earthenware pots has been a well-developed industry since ancient times. Even now, porous unglazed pitchers and jars are still used in both rural and urban areas to keep drinking water, not only in homes but in streets and lanes for thirsty passers-by. In the hot summer weather, this is a traditional way of cooling water: it seeps through the porous clay and evaporates, cooling the surface of the pot and the water in it. The small pot is called a *qulla*, the medium-sized one with a handle, also used in the home, is the *jarra*, while the large pitcher on a stand in the street is a *zir*. Their capacity ranges from three to fifteen liters.

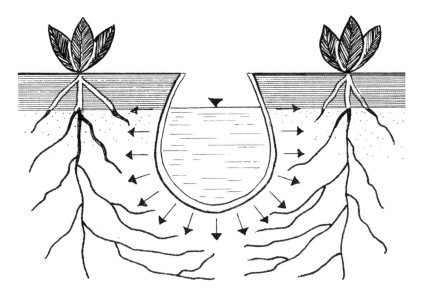

Figure 19: The clay pot buried in the soil and filled with water. Arrows show water penetrating the porous walls of the clay pot into the soil.

The size of the pot to be used in irrigation varies according to that of the plants. Small plants with shallow roots will obviously need smaller pots, as in the case of desert grasses and annual plants. For irrigating under-shrubs and shrubs with well-developed roots larger pots are required. When larger pots are used less frequent irrigation is needed.

In Wadi Allaqi field station a pitcher containing ten liters of water was used to irrigate a lime tree that was growing inside the courtyard. Water sufficient to maintain the growth of the tree was added weekly or even every second week, depending on the weather conditions and stage of growth. The shape of the pots varied. The flat-bottomed small pots were suitable for those plants whose roots could easily spread under them. However, the larger *zir,* similar in shape to the ancient oval amphora with its pointed bottom, increases the area which is in contact with the roots and is easy to bury in the soil.

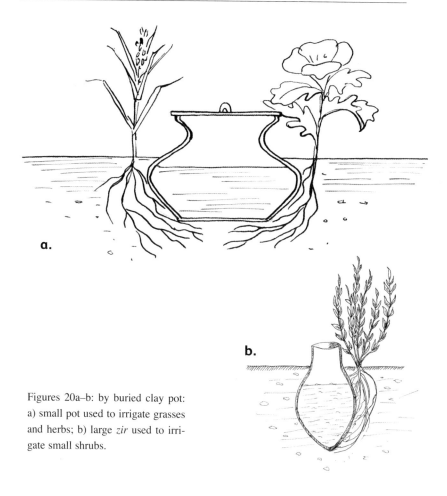

Figures 20a–b: by buried clay pot:
a) small pot used to irrigate grasses
and herbs; b) large *zir* used to irrigate small shrubs.

Also of significance is the size of the mouth. If it is large, it is easier to
add water to the pot, but if the opening is not covered, the water will
quickly evaporate. In addition, a lid will have to be made, adding to the
cost. The narrow-mouthed pitcher is more difficult to fill by hand with
water, but is easier to cover, even with a stone or piece of rock, and plants
can easily be planted near the oval-shaped and narrow-mouthed jars. Lids
should fully cover the top of the pot; poorly fitted covers may enable unde-
sirable insects, reptiles, and small mammals to slip in.

The upper part of the clay pot can be painted either with plastic paint or varnish to reduce water use and bring water close to the root zone. This is recommended for the cultivation of plants with deep roots. Pots can either be filled with water by hand or hose or connected to a pipe network.

A hole should first be dug of a size suitable for both burying the pot and planting the plant. In sandy soil, which is characteristic of most desert soil, the bottom should be covered with a layer of clay. This will store any excess of water and prevent water loss. The top of the buried pot should be a few centimeters above the soil surface. The buried clay pot should be filled regularly and kept from becoming completely dry.

The most common mistake made is to place the plant too far from the clay pot, outside the zone of the wetted soil.

Vertical pipe irrigation

A simple subsurface irrigation system was designed and tested in the experimental farm located in Wadi Allaqi Biosphere Reserve. This irrigation design is based on ecological studies of desert plants in their natural habitats. It is recommended for deeply rooted desert plants and is best suited for garden areas where underground water is available at a depth that could be reached by the roots of the trees. Taking into consideration that the roots of many desert trees can penetrate to a depth of ten to twenty meters, such areas are ideal for the establishment of gardens.

Expensive tools and equipment are not required for this form of irrigation, which is easily installed. The essential components are PVC tubes, open at both ends, and a tool such as an auger to dig the soil. Both the length and the diameter of the tube may vary in size according to factors like the type of soil, the landscape features, plants, and water availability.

In the irrigation system that has already been tested, PVC tubes (four-inch diameter) with a length of one-and-a-half meters were vertically installed in the ground to the depth of one meter, while half a meter of the tube remained above the surface.

If the ground is difficult to dig, a smaller length of tube can be used, but this will need to be filled with water more frequently. Water can either be added manually or pipeline tubes (similar to drip irrigation) could be connected to form a network.

Seedlings should be planted at a distance of not more than twenty centimeters from the tube. It is advisable to use seedlings of trees or young plants that are eight to ten months, but not less than five months old.

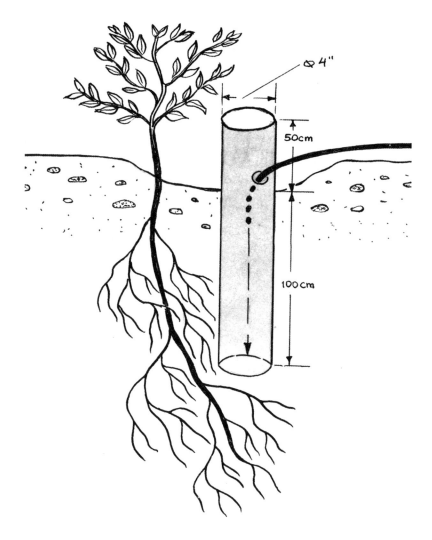

Figure 21: Vertical pipe method of irrigation used in Wadi Allaqi experimental farm to grow indigenous desert trees.

For three to four months after planting, seedlings should be irrigated manually by adding water to the soil surface directly at the plant's base. After the plant has become well established and new foliage has appeared, water should be added to the tube weekly, filling it to the top. If the tubes have a ten-centimeter diameter and a length of 150 cm, each tree receives about twelve liters of water each time it is irrigated. In such a water regime, 200 trees planted in one acre will receive about ten cubic meters of water monthly (Springuel 2001).

The percolation of water downwards through the sandy soil will facilitate the elongation of the roots. As soon as the roots reach the underground water, irrigation can be stopped. Another advantage of this method of irrigation is that it prevents salinization of the soil.

8

Plant Descriptions

Trees and shrubs[26]

Acacia Mill.

Family Leguminosae, subfamily Mimosoidea

Acacia trees could become the keystone species in the garden design. There are about 1200 *Acacia* species, of which the majority are found in tropical and subtropical regions in Australia, Africa, and America. The spineless Australian acacias are introduced to arid regions all over the world and cultivated for different purposes.

Many leguminous species, including acacias, have nodules on their roots with nitrogen-fixing bacteria (legume-*Rhizobium* symbiotic system) which enrich soil with nitrogen. This is especially important for desert soils which are poor in nutrients, particularly nitrogen, and it also helps acacias survive in dry conditions.

There are ten *Acacia* species, two of which have two subspecies, which are indigenous in Egypt (Boulos 1999–2005, v. 3), plus *Faidherbia albida*, which is very close to the *Acacia* genus and is more commonly known by the name white acacia or apple ring acacia *(Acacia albida)*.

Acacias grow throughout Egypt but are most plentiful in the south of the country, because this area represents the northern limits of geographical distribution for some acacias *(Acacia seyal, Acacia laeta)* which penetrated to Egypt through the Nile Valley from the savanna belt in the southern Sahel. There are many acacias in the Gebel Elba mountains group in the southeastern corner of Egypt, which receive a frequent misty rain that originates at high altitudes. *Acacia pachyceras* grows only in the central and eastern parts of Sinai and nowhere else in Egypt.

According to their water requirements, acacias in Egypt are divided into two groups: those that require more water and grow in the Nile Valley (*A. seyal, A. laeta, A. nilotica*) and the drought-resistant desert acacias (*A. tortilis* subsp. *raddiana*, *A. tortilis* subsp. *tortilis, A. pachyceras* and *A. ehrenbergiana*,). However, even in the desert, the acacias growing there prefer habitats with relatively high amounts of water, i.e., the low-lying area or the drainage system (the desert wadis) where rainwater collects from an extensive rocky plateau and is stored in the wadi-fill deposits.

Faidherbia albida has special ecological requirements. It usually grows in the Nile Valley and can withstand a long period of inundation, as commonly happens on the shores of Lake Nasser. It can also grow in desert wadis.

Evidence of the pharaonic appreciation of acacias is well documented in inscriptions and wall paintings in tombs. Many items of everyday life found in the tombs were made from acacia wood. However, one of the most fascinating artifacts reflecting awareness of the role played by the acacia in nature is the famous Twelfth Dynasty Beni Hassan depiction of an acacia tree with identifiable birds, which is now in the Egyptian Museum.

Figure 22: Drawing after a section of wall painting in Twelfth Dynasty Beni Hassan tomb in the Egyptian Museum, showing a hoopoe on an acacia tree. Drawing by Nadia Kotb.

Most of the indigenous acacias can be recommended for use in landscaping/desert gardening. For the selection of the acacia trees described in this book, the following criteria were taken into consideration:
- species which play a significant role in the natural ecosystem (keystone plants), so that, once established, they will create microhabitats suitable for other biota;
- species with a broad range of ecological amplitude, allowing cultivation of plants in different parts of Egypt in ecologically favorable habitats;
- species which are threatened because of habitat loss, and need human intervention to ensure their population survival;
- and, of course the aesthetic values provided by shape, rich blooms and attractive fragrance.

According to these criteria the following acacias are recommended for cultivation in desert gardens: *Acacia nilotica; Acacia laeta; Acacia mellifera; Acacia ehrenbergiana; Acacia tortilis* subsp. *raddiana; Acacia tortilis* subsp. *tortilis; Acacia seyal; Acacia pachyceras* (syn. *Acacia gerrardii*), and *Faidherbia albida* (syn. *Acacia albida*).

In some publications *Acacia tortilis* subsp. *raddiana* and *Acacia tortilis* subsp. *tortilis* are described as two separate species (*Acacia tortilis* and *Acacia raddiana*) because they differ in their appearance, phenology (time of flowering and fruiting), and genetic characters[27] that we should consider for landscaping purposes.

The above-mentioned acacia species are easily distinguished one from another, even by non-specialists, by means of the arrangement of the flowers in the inflorescence (flower cluster). The flowers of *Acacia laeta*, *A. mellifera* and *Faidherbia albida* are arranged in a flowering spike while in other species flowers form a globular flowering head. Twigs of acacias are armed with sharp outgrowths of either spines (spinescent) or prickles (non-spinescent).[28] Among acacias listed above, both *A. laeta* and *A. mellifera* are non-spinescent, while other acacias are spinescent. All acacias in Egypt have bipinnate leaves, i.e., feather-like compound leaves divided into leaflets, but a distinguishing characteristic is the varying number of pinnae and leaflets in different species. Fruits of acacias are called pods, which vary in size, shape, color, and number of seeds. When they are mature, the pods of some acacias split open to release the enclosed seeds, but the pods of *Acacia nilotica*, *A. pachyceras*, *A. tortilis* and *Faidherbia albida* do not split and the seeds remain inside the pods.

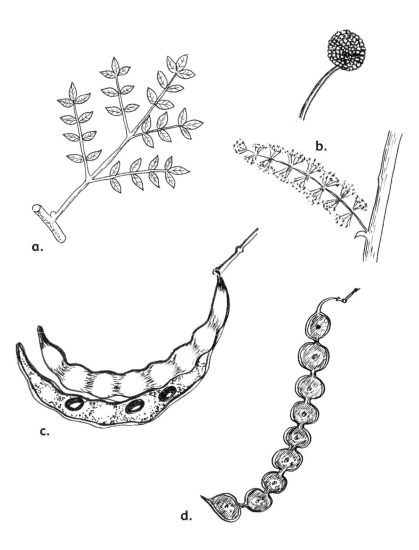

Figures 23a–d: a) Bipinnate leaves showing pinnae with leaflets; b) inflorescences in spike (top) and heads (bottom); c) split pod with ripe seeds; and d) a pod remaining closed containing ripe seeds.

Propagation of acacias

All acacias recommended in this book can be grown from seeds; in fact the germination of seeds is the most practicable method for the propagation of acacias. In spite of some specific differences between plants, there are common recommendations that can be given for their preparation for cultivation.

Seeds should be collected as soon as they ripen. The fruits of many acacias are often damaged by insects, which lay eggs within the seeds even before they mature. Acacias growing in the desert, e.g., *Acacia ehrenbergiana*, are more easily infected by insects than trees growing in the Nile Valley. Vogt (1995) recommends separating the seeds infected by insects by floating them off in water.

As soon as fruits mature in some acacias (*A. ehrenbergiana*, *A. seyal*, *A. mellifera*, and *A. laeta*), they split along the midrib and their seeds are dispersed, adding to difficulty of seed collection. Seeds remain inside the legume in other acacias, but many are still infected while they remain on the tree.

While collected, the seeds should be first separated from the pods and stored in a cold dry place. The best temperature for the germination of most acacias is between 20°C and 30°C. Seeds of acacias germinate better if the hard coat covering the seeds is broken before they are put in the soil. This can be broken mechanically either with a knife or with emery paper, ensuring that the embryo is not damaged. Results will be better if the seeds are first soaked in warm water (50°–60°C) for one hour.

Pre-treated seeds should be sown in a plastic bag or in a clay pot filled to two-thirds of its volume with soil mixture (two parts sand to one part silt). Use plastic bags or pots which are at least 30 cm deep to allow for taproot development. A small opening should be made in plastic bags for drainage of excess water. Sow two or three seeds in each pot and, when the seeds germinate, pull out the weakest seedling(s) to leave only the strongest. Water to keep soil in the pot moist, but take care not to over-water plants to ensure good aeration in the soil, which is important for root growth. The plants' subsequent water requirements vary according to the local climate, for example in hot and dry Upper Egypt they should be watered three times per week in summer and twice in week in winter. The seedlings may be planted in the ground when they are from four to six months old. They may actually be kept in pots until they are one year old, but no longer, as after this time the taproot may protrude through the container.

The best time to plant out seedlings is February to March, in a pre-dug hole from fifty to seventy centimeters deep. If the soil is light and sandy, it is recommended that a layer of silt or heavier soil be placed at the bottom of the hole, followed by some manure or compost, and covered with sand. Carefully remove the plant from the plastic bag without disturbing the root, then place it in the hole and cover with soil. The newly planted young plants should be watered frequently, every other day for the first month. Further watering of the plants depends on the local conditions: prevailing temperature, type of soil, depth of underground water, topography, proximity to a water body, irrigation system used and water requirement of each species. Three acacias (*A. seyal, A. nilotica,* and *A. laeta*) are water-loving plants and will need more frequent watering compared with drought resistant acacias (*A. raddiana, A. tortilis,* and *A. ehrenbergiana*). Common to all is that the more water you give, the faster the plants will grow, but the ground should not be waterlogged, particularly if the ground water is close to the surface.

Acacia ehrenbergiana Hayne [29] (Pl. 1)

English: no recorded name

Arabic: *salam, selem*

Distribution: widespread in the western and central Sahara, extending to Arabia.

Distribution in Egypt: common in the driest parts of the southern part of the Eastern Desert; occurs in the oases of the Western Desert.

Habitat: *salam* is the most drought resistant of the acacias growing in Egypt. It usually grows on desert plains covered by deep layers of sand, on sandy soils in the broad wadis, and in rocky habitats. It can tolerate very high temperatures and heavy browsing by animals.

Historical records: *A. ehrenbergiana* has the strongest wood of all the acacias. In ancient times, pieces of this wood were used to break up rocks containing ornamental stones, such as granite and marble. Dry pieces of acacia wood were inserted in holes in the rock and watered; their expansion split the rocks into small pieces.

Plant uses: an excellent plant for fuel because it produces more heat and is slower burning than the other acacias. It is especially good for preparing *gabana,* the traditional Bedouin coffee. Its leaves and small branches are very nutritious, so it is important as fodder for livestock. Because it usually grows as a shrub, animals can easily reach the soft parts of the plant. The staff which is an essential part of the Bedouin's equipment, is almost always made from the slender straight twigs of this acacia.

Life form: evergreen shrub; it rarely has the appearance of a tree. Sheds leaves in prolonged dry periods.

Root: develops very deep taproot and widely spread lateral roots.

Stem: it is multi-stemmed, starting from the base. The stem is slender, covered by grayish-brown bark, which sometimes peels, revealing the smooth inner layer. It has long, slender, sharp spines, which are usually longer than its leaves. Characteristic of this acacia are galls made by insects and attached to twigs. They look like spines but are white and soft to the touch. Leaves are in one or two pinnae pairs with 8 to 10 leaflets per pinna. Flowers are in heads, light yellow with a sweet smell. The flowering period is from March until the end of April.

Crown: the several stems of this acacia provide the irregular shape of its crown, with twigs pointing straight up giving a characteristic fountain-like appearance to the shrub.

Fruits: pods are reddish-brown, smooth, long (up to 8 cm), slender, containing 5 to 7 seeds. In May, the ripe pods split along the mid rib to release the seeds, which are very quickly infected by insects.

Regeneration: by seeds.

Availability of propagules: seeds should be collected in the wild as soon as they ripen, before they become infected by insects.

Propagation: to enhance germination the seeds are dropped into hot water and soaked overnight.

Figure 24: *Acacia ehrenbergiana*: flowering branch and fruits. Drawing by Irina Lavrova.

Acacia laeta R. Br. exBenth[30] (Pl. 2)

English: no recorded name

Arabic: *hashaab*

Distribution: *Acacia laeta* extends from Central Africa (Burkina Faso, Niger) eastwards to the Red Sea in Sudan and the south of Egypt. In Asia, it occurs in Iraq, Yemen, and Saudi Arabia.

Distribution in Egypt: the northern limit of its geographical distribution is in the southern part of Egypt. Its natural growth is limited to a small population, comprising only a few individuals, still growing on the First Cataract Islands at Aswan. A few trees, most probably cultivated, can also be seen in old gardens in Aswan. A sparse growth of *Acacia laeta* has been recorded on the Gebel Elba Mountains on the Egyptian border with Sudan.

Habitat: it usually grows near rivers and in places with ground water close to the surface on rocky habitats. This tree can tolerate different substrata from heavy silt to rocks, and high air temperature.

Plant uses: its timber is good as a building material and fuel. The gum is edible and sold commercially in Sudan.

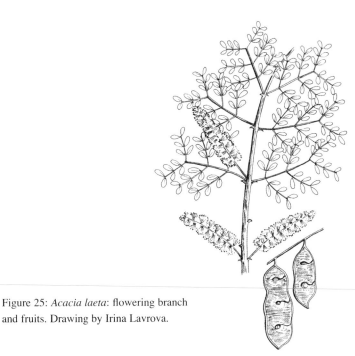

Figure 25: *Acacia laeta*: flowering branch and fruits. Drawing by Irina Lavrova.

71

Life form: the tree remains evergreen with a sufficient water supply, and sheds its leaves when there is a scarcity of water.

Stem: can reach a height of up to 10 meters. There is a single stem with a diameter of 75 to 100 cm in old trees. The leaves are bipinnate, pinnae 2 to 3 pairs, each with 3 to 5 pairs of leaflets. The flowers are white in long spikes. They begin flowering at the end of winter, usually in February.

Crown: irregular, becomes more rounded and dense with age.

Fruits: the pod is thin and flat, from dark to light brown with 2–3 seeds.

Regeneration: by seeds.

Availability of propagules: seeds can be collected from the First Cataract Islands at Aswan. The request for seeds should be sent to the EEAA Administration of Saluga and Ghazel Conservation Islands in Aswan.

Propagation: fresh seeds germinate well without special treatment, but for faster germination, soaking in hot water for 12 hours is recommended.

Planting in the ground: seedlings grow fast, and should be planted out when they are 4–5 months old.

Note: the young trees grow very slowly in desert conditions and much faster in the Nile Valley.

Acacia mellifera (Vahl) Benth.[31] (Pl. 3)

English: hook thorn (Kenya), wait a bit thorn (Sudan), black thorn (South Africa)

Arabic: *haashab, tekkeer, kitr*

Distribution: Arabia extending to northeast and southwest Africa.

Distribution in Egypt: limited, growing on the Red Sea Hills and in the Gebel Elba mountains.

Habitat: grows on hills and mountains at altitudes up to 1500 meters and prefers rocky and heavy soils. It can tolerate high temperatures. It has often been recorded as forming impenetrable thickets in favorable conditions.

Plant uses: good for fuel. However, it has a limited value for making charcoal because of its sparse distribution in Egypt where it usually grows as a shrub or small tree and has a low wood production. Vogt (1995) gives an account of uses of this plant in African countries, where its roots are used in making baskets, its branches for fencing, and the pods and leaves are good fodder for livestock. Different parts of the plant are used in traditional medicine for the treatment of various disorders such as stomach pain, sore eyes, pneumonia, malaria, and many others.

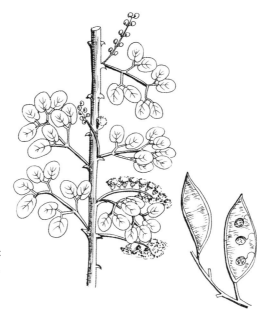

Figure 26: *Acacia mellifera*:
flowering branch and fruits.
Drawing by Irina Lavrova.

Life form: evergreen shrub or small tree, which usually shed its leaves in the dry period.

Root: roots deeply penetrate into cracks between the rocks where rainfall water is stored. Nico Smit, in his book *Guide to Acacia of South Africa* (1999), reproduces a magnificent photo of *A. mellifera*, showing excavated lateral roots of the tree extensively spreading in the surface soil layer. These roots enable the tree to survive in areas with a low rainfall and also allow it to compete successfully with other plants for water and nutrients.

Stem: multi-stemmed, and can reach a height of up to 6 meters but usually is about 3 to 4 meters high. The stem is covered by grayish-brown to dark purplish-brown bark. Pairs of hooked gray or yellow prickles occur on the branches near the nodes where the leaves are attached. Leaves are very distinct in two pairs of pinnae, each with only 1 to 3 pairs of leaflets, which are larger than in other acacias. Mellifluous (honeyed) white to cream flowers are in spikes, attracting bees and sunbirds, hence the species name *mellifera*.

Crown: the branches grow from low down the stem, and can even reach the ground, forming a broad crown, rounded to flattened in shape.

Fruits: pods are flat, short, and broad, tapering at both ends, and light brown, usually with 2 to 3 seeds.

Regeneration: by seeds.

Availability of propagules: seeds can be obtained in wild from the Gebel Elba Protected Area with permission from the EEAA.

Propagation: seeds germinate easily without pre-treatment in 3 to 5 days. After growing for about 5 months in the nursery, seedlings can be planted into the ground. Heavy silt or clay soil is the most suitable for growing this tree.

Acacia nilotica (L.) Delile[32] (Pl. 4)

English: Nile acacia, Egyptian thorn

Arabic: *sant, sont*

Distribution: the Nile acacia is widely distributed throughout the northern African continent, extending to Asia in India and Pakistan.

Distribution in Egypt: mainly grows in the Nile Valley and in the oases of the Western Desert. It can often be seen along the irrigation canals and roads, where it provides shade on hot summer days.

Habitat: moist places beside water pools in oases, the banks of the River Nile, and irrigation canals. It can withstand long periods of inundation and survive up to three years on the shores of Lake Nasser, while flooded by water rising from the lake. The trees are also able to tolerate short drought periods and soil salinity, but in response to both stresses shed their leaves.

Figure 27: *Acacia nilotica*: flowering branch and fruits. Drawing by Irina Lavrova.

Historical records: "In Pharaonic times the wood was used for timber, the bark for tanning and the leaves, flowers, and pods found multiple uses in medicine" (Manniche 1999). Nile acacia, growing close to the river, was probably the main source of wood for pharaonic boat construction, taking into consideration that it has been continuously used for the same purpose until the present (Hepper 1990). Pods of Nile acacia found in Old Kingdom tombs are displayed at the Egyptian Agricultural Museum in Doqqi and its flowers are a component of pharaonic garlands kept in the Egyptian Antiquities Museum and Agricultural Museum (Hamdi 2003).

Plant uses: every part of this tree is intensively used. Wood of the Nile acacia is hard, good for carving and turnery, and used for making many different tools. Its alleged resistance to termites is doubtful: different sources provide divergent information. It is excellent for fuel and charcoal and provides good quality gum arabic, which was commercially extracted from this acacia in the past. Leaves and specially pods are nutritious and very valuable as fodder for livestock. Vogt (1995) mentions that in some African countries the gum, green pods, and seeds are consumed: the seeds should be roasted before being eaten. The bark and pods contain tannins, which are widely used in the tanning of leather, while the pods are sometimes used for making dyes (yellow, red, and black). Different parts of the tree are used in traditional medicine, particularly in Upper Egypt; the pods with enclosed seeds are popular for treating coughs.

Life form: evergreen tree

Root: forms intensive lateral roots. Its taproot can penetrate to a depth of up to 5 to 6 meters and reach the subsurface water.

Stem: it is a single-stemmed tree of 7 to 10 meters high. The bark of mature trees is rough, dark with longitudinal fissures. The paired spines at the base of each leaf are very noticeable; they are straight to slightly curved and white in color. Leaves are bipinnate, number of pinnae pairs range from 5 to 10, with leaflets from 7 to 12 per pinnae. The rounded flowering heads are bright yellow and sweet-scented.

Crown: branching is from low down the stem with horizontal spread twigs forming a compact rounded crown, which provides good shade.

Fruits: pods are long with marked constrictions between the seeds. The immature pods are green, changing to dark brown when ripe. The pods break up transversely into single-seeded segments, remaining on the tree for almost a year with the seeds still inside, before falling.

Regeneration: by seeds.

Availability of propagules: seeds are easy to collect from trees, which are common in Nile Valley rural areas. Pods *(karad)* are usually sold in plant markets in cities and towns throughout Egypt. Seeds should be removed from the pod and examined well to select only good, non-infected seeds.

Propagation: pre-treatment is needed to break the seed coat for seed to germinate. A good way to soften the seed coat is to put seeds in boiling water, then leave them to soak for 24 hours. In some rural areas, the pods are fed to goats and the scarified seeds are removed from their droppings. Seeds should be sown directly after treatment, in containers filled with a mixture of sand and silt. The seedlings are ready for planting out after 5 to 6 months.

Acacia pachyceras O. Schwartz[33] (Pl. 5)

Syn. *Acacia gerrardii* Benth.

English: Acacia

Arabic: no recorded name

Distribution: Oman, Kuwait, Saudi Arabia, southern Iraq, and Palestine.

Distribution in Egypt: only in the central and eastern part of Sinai.

Habitat: alluvial deposits in the wadis that dissect the gravelly plains of central and eastern Sinai.

Plant uses: because of its limited distribution in Egypt, this plant is used only locally in Sinai. Its wood is good for charcoal and often used by Bedouins for fuel.

Life form: evergreen tree.

Root: develops a long taproot.

Stem: single trunk is up to 7 meters in height, with a diameter of about 60 cm. The bark of mature trees is rough, dark gray or brown, longitudinally fissured. The stems of young trees are smooth, varying in color from light gray to red-brown, with long sharp spines, which may attain a length of 10 cm. The pair of spines at the base of the leaves is straight or slightly curved and white in color. Leaves are bipinnate, pinnae in 6 to 8 pairs, with leaflets of up to 28 pairs. Flowers are arranged in heads, white or yellowish in color with a pleasant smell.

Crown: branching occurs high up the trunk, forming a sparse, slightly flattish crown.

Fruits: pods are borne either singly or in a small bunch. They are long and narrow, about 10 cm in length and 1 cm broad, 8 to 10 seeds, sickle-shaped and covered with short velvety gray hairs.

Regeneration: by seeds

Figure 28: *Acacia pachyceras*: flowering (top) and fruiting branches. Drawing by Irina Lavrova.

Availability of propagules: seeds can be collected in the wild in Sinai. For assistance in obtaining seedlings and saplings of *Acacia pachyceras* contact Dina Aly.[34]

Propagation: for good germination, pre-treatment of seeds is needed. Scratching the seed coat gives a good germination of almost 90 percent; however, it should be done very carefully, in order not to damage the embryo. Soaking of seeds in sulfuric acid for 20 minutes, followed by washing in running water, also gives good results.

Acacia seyal Delile[35] (Pl. 6)

English: no recorded name

Arabic: *talh*, *sayaal*

Distribution: widely distributed throughout the arid African countries from Senegal in the west to Sudan in the east and from Namibia and Mozambique in the south to Egypt in the north.

Distribution in Egypt: typical Sahelian tree, which has penetrated Egypt through the Nile Valley and grows in the southern part of Egypt on the Nile banks between Aswan and Luxor. It also grows on the First Cataract Islands at Aswan where it forms dense thickets.

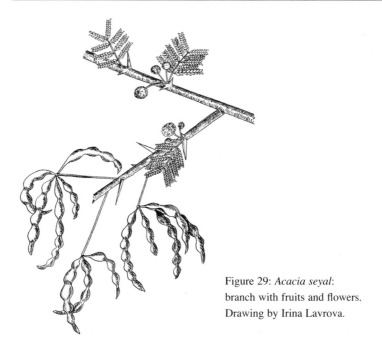

Figure 29: *Acacia seyal*:
branch with fruits and flowers.
Drawing by Irina Lavrova.

Habitat: prefers a hot climate and heavy silt soil, but can also grow on rocks where pockets of soil are available. In the South Valley University desert garden at Aswan, this acacia grows very well on sandy soil, which is frequently irrigated. When it occurs on the Nile banks, it can tolerate short episodes of inundation.

Historical records: its flowers were used in garlands and bouquets, which have been found in pharaonic tombs (Hamdi 2003).

Plant uses: it is good for firewood, as are most acacias, and charcoal production, and provides good fodder for livestock. A commercial gum is produced from this tree in Sudan. Different parts of this plant are used in traditional medicine. For example, the bark of *A. seyal*, when added to water, kills the freshwater snails that carry the bilharzia parasite. The smoke produced by burning the wood of *Acacia seyal* acts as a fumigant against insects and lice; it is also believed that exposure to the smoke relieves rheumatic pains. The gum is used in medicine against colds and diarrhea.

Life form: evergreen tree, usually 7 meters high, but in favorable conditions can grow up to 12 meters.

Plate 1: *Acacia ehrenbergiana*, tree in bloom and flowering branch, Wadi Allaqi, April 2005. Photographs by Irina Springuel. (p.69)

Plate 2: *Acacia laeta*, young tree in the desert garden, university campus, Aswan, May 2003, with flowering and fruiting branches. Photographs by Irina Springuel. (p.71)

Plate 3: *Acacia mellifera*, small trees, with fruiting branches, at Gebel Elba. Photographs courtesy of Cultnat. (p.72)

Plate 4: *Acacia nilotica*, crown of tree growing in Aswan, with flowering and fruiting branches in the Dina Aly garden, December 2005. Photographs by Magdi Radi and Irina Springuel. (p.74)

Plate 5: *Acacia pachyceras*, crown of young tree with fruits in the Dina Aly garden, a young tree's bark with spines, and a small branch with leaves, December 2005. Photographs by Irina Springuel. (p.76)

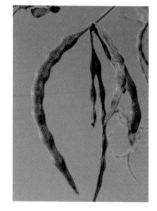

Plate 6: *Acacia seyal*, tree in bloom, the desert garden, university campus, Aswan, May 2004, with fruits and flowers. Photographs by Irina Springuel. (p.77)

Plate 7: *Acacia tortilis* subsp. *tortilis*, young tree in the Dina Aly garden. Photograph by Irina Springuel. (p.79)

Plate 8: *Acacia tortilis* subsp. *raddiana* tree in the upstream part of Wadi Allaqi, Eastern Desert. Photograph by Irina Springuel. (p.81)

Plate 9: *Faidherbia albida*, tree grown in the desert garden on the university campus in Aswan, and flowering and fruiting branches. Photographs by Irina Springuel and Magdi Radi. (p.83)

Plate 10: *Balanites aegyptiaca*, four-year old tree in the desert garden, university campus, Aswan, and branch with thorns and fruits, December 2005. Photographs by Magdi Radi and Irina Springuel. (p.85)

Plate 11: *Calotropis procera*, tree growing in the wild, Gebel Elba. Photograph courtesy of Cultnat. Branch bearing fruits and flowers in the university desert garden, Aswan. Photographs by Irina Springuel. (p.88)

Plate 12: *Capparis decidua*, tree with flowering and fruiting branches growing in the upstream part of Wadi Allaqi. Photographs by Magdi Radi and Irina Springuel. (p.90)

Plate 13: *Ficus sycomorus*, four-year-old tree in the Dina Aly garden. Photograph by Irina Springuel. Ripe fruits. Courtesy of Cultnat. (p.91)

Plate 14: *Maerua crassifolia*, tree in the upstream part of Wadi Allaqi with flowering branch and fruits. Photographs by Irina Springuel and Magdi Radi. (p.94)

Plate 15: *Moringa peregrina*, tree in the Orman Garden, Giza. Flowers on tree in the Eastern Desert. Branch with flowering buds and seedling grown in the Dina Aly garden. Photographs by Irina Springuel and Rafik Khalil and Dina Aly. (p.96)

Plate 16: *Olea europaea* subsp.
europaea, olive tree on the North
(Mediterranean) Coast, with fruiting
branch, December 2005. Photographs
by Irina Springuel. (p.97)

Plate 17: *Salvadora persica*, an old bush in Wadi Allaqi and detail of its branch with fruits. Photographs by Irina Springuel and Magdi Radi. (p.100)

Plate 18: *Sesbania sesban*, crown of young tree in the desert garden, university campus, Aswan, and flowering and fruiting branches. Photographs by Magdi Radi. (p.102)

Plate 19: *Tamarix aphylla*, tree on the North (Mediterranean) Coast, and young trees and close-up of crown in the Wadi Allaqi experimental farm. Photographs by Irina Springuel. (p.104)

Plate 20: *Ziziphus spina-christi*, roadside tree in Aswan, with fruiting branch. Photographs by Irina Springuel. (p.107)

Plate 21: *Draceana ombet*, tree growing on the mountain slopes at Gebel Elba. Courtesy of Cultnat. (p.109)

Plate 22: *Hyphaene thebaica*, doum palm growing beside the road leading to Aswan Dam. Photograph by Irina Springuel. Doum fruits from Dungul Oasis, November 2005. Photograph by Magdi Radi. (p.110)

Plate 23: *Medemia argun*, fruiting palm and young individuals in the background at Dungul oasis, and fruits and a cross-section of the seed, November 2005. Photograph by Magdi Radi. (p.113)

Plate 24: *Phoenix dactylif-era*, date palm growing in Kharga Oasis, Western Desert, and the palm's crown with immature green fruits. Photographs by Hala Barakat. (p.115)

Plate 25: *Calligonum poly-gonoides*, small shrub with small white flowers and red fruits in the Western Desert. Photograph by Rafik Khalil and Dina Aly. (p.117)

Plate 26: *Capparis spinosa*, close-up of the flowering plant in Southern Sinai. Photograph by Rafik Khalil and Dina Aly. (p.119)

Plate 27: *Leptadenia pyrotechnica*, heavily grazed shrub in the upstream part of Wadi Allaqi, with flowering branch and fruits. Photographs by Irina Springuel and Magdi Radi. (p.121)

Plate 28: *Nerium oleander.* Photograph by Magdi Radi. (p.122)

Plate 29: *Senna alexandrina*, flowering and fruiting branches of a shrub grown in the desert garden, university campus, Aswan, December 2005. Photograph by Magdi Radi. (p.128)

Plate 30: *Retama raetam*, flowering shrub (center) in the Dina Aly garden, and fruiting branch and close-up of the delicate flowers. Photographs by Irina Springuel. (p.124)

Plate 31: *Ricinus communis*, plant growing in the university desert garden, Aswan, and branch bearing immature fruits at the top and male flowers on the lower part of the inflorescence. Photograph by Magdi Radi. (p.126)

Plate 32: *Solenostemma arghel*, shrub with fruits and flowers in the university desert garden, Aswan, and flowering branch and branch bearing immature fruits. Photographs by Magdi Radi and Irina Springuel. (p.129)

Plate 33: *Anastatica hierochuntica*, wooden tub piled high with dry curled-up plants collected from the desert on sale in Aswan market, and dried-up plant in its natural desert habitat. Photographs by Magdi Radi and Irina Springuel. (p.132)

Plate 34: *Datura innoxia*, annual plant growing in the wild in Aswan, with the flowering branch and immature fruit. Photographs by Magdi Radi and Irina Springuel. (p.134)

Plate 35: *Arundo donax*, grass growing on the North (Mediterranean) coast, and close-up of its inflorescence. Photographs by Irina Springuel. (p.135)

Plate 36: Self-sown *Cymbopogon schoenanthus* subsp. *proximus*, grass in the desert garden at the university campus in Aswan, and the flowering inflorescences. Photographs by Magdi Radi. (p.137)

Stem: diameter of the main trunk of mature trees can reach one meter. The bark is smooth, cream to greenish-yellow in color, covered by the orange-red powder that is the distinguishing characteristic of this tree. The long spines, which are usually straight and paired, occur densely both on the branches and the main stem. The leaves are bipinnate, in 3 to 6 pairs of pinnae with 8 to 12 pairs of leaflets. Flowers are sweet smelling, with bright yellow rounded heads.

Crown: there is branching low down on the stem forming a broad, widely spread crown.

Fruits: the seeds (10 to 14) are in long slender pods, brown when mature, which are slightly curved in clusters. When mature, the pods split and release the seeds while the clusters of pods remain on the tree long after the seeds have dispersed. Seeds ripen in the late spring or at the beginning of summer.

Regeneration: by seeds.

Availability of propagules: Seeds can be collected in the wild from the First Cataract Islands at Aswan. The request for seeds should be sent to the EEAA administration of Saluga and Ghazel Conservation Islands in Aswan.

Propagation: The easiest way of propagation is by seeds. Pre-treatment is needed for optimum germination; the simplest method is to nick the seed coat or dip it briefly into boiling water. Seedlings grow fast and can be ready for transplanting from the nursery into the ground after five months. Vogt (1995) states that this tree can be reproduced from cuttings.

Acacia tortilis subsp. *tortilis* (Forssk.) Hayne[36] (Pl. 7)

English: umbrella thorn

Arabic: *samoor*

Distribution: widespread in sub-Saharan Africa from Mauritania to Sudan and in East Africa from Ethiopia to South Africa. In Asia, it is found in Israel, Saudi Arabia, and Yemen, and extends to dry areas in India.

Distribution in Egypt: this acacia grows in the southern part of the Eastern Desert, in wadis which drain the Red Sea Hills and along the seashore, in the Gebel Elba region and the southern part of Sinai.

Habitat: it is a salt-resistant plant. However, on very saline soil, usually close to the sea, its height is about 2 to 4 meters, while on non-saline soil trees are usually above 10 meters high. It prefers hot weather and low altitude. Surviving in the starkest sites, it is a promising species for afforesting dry, rocky, and sandy areas.

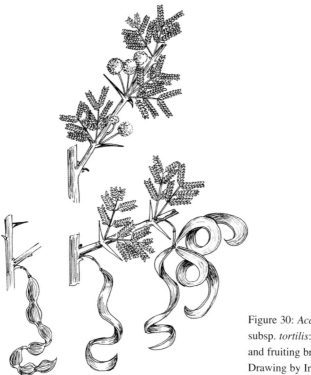

Figure 30: *Acacia tortilis*
subsp. *tortilis*: flowering (top)
and fruiting branches.
Drawing by Irina Lavrova.

Plant uses: growing in severe conditions where other plants cannot survive, this tree is the most valuable resource for all desert inhabitants. It offers shelter from the burning sun. Its foliage and pods are very nutritious, providing food for both domestic and wild animals in dry periods. The wood is solid and used for manufacturing small implements. It has a high calorific value and makes superior firewood and charcoal. It is an excellent tree for stabilizing the soil.

Life form: it is an evergreen tree but can shed leaves during prolonged drought and under high salinity stress. It can grow as a shrub in saline soils on the Red Sea coast.

Root: the taproot penetrates down 20 to 25 meters where a wet soil layer or underground water is available. It also produces lateral surface roots, which collect water from a large surface area around the tree.

Stem: the trees or shrubs, often with a few stems, rise from the base covered by rough and fissured dark gray bark. Trees growing in the desert are 5 to 10 meters high with a diameter of up to 60 cm; along the seashore, they are much shorter, growing as shrubs about 2 to 3 meters high. Both short hooked and long straight spines appear on the leaf base. Young branches and leaves are pubescent (covered with tiny hairs). Leaves are bipinnate, pinnae in 3 to 6 pairs with 7 to 10 pairs of leaflets. Flowers are white or pale-yellow, borne in round clusters, flowering in late spring.
Crown: the umbrella shaped crown is not very compact and is flat-topped.
Fruits: the pods split and release seeds when they are ripe. The hairy and twisted pods are yellowish-brown when ripe, 7 to 11 cm long, with 4 to 7 seeds that usually ripen in summer.
Regeneration: by seeds.
Availability of propagules: seeds can be collected in the wild from the natural habitats. Because pods and seeds of *A. tortilis* are very similar to *A. raddiana*, take care that the seeds collected are from an *A. tortilis* tree.
Propagation: for the best germination, mechanical abrasion of the seed coat is recommended, or seeds can be soaked for 24 hours in warm water prior to cultivation. Seeds germinate best at a temperature of about 30°C. For the best results, seeds should be germinated in pods or plastic bags filled with sandy soil (3 parts of sand to 1 part of silt). Seedlings grow fast when watered well but should not become water-logged.
Comments: with its dense and spreading flat crown, it makes an attractive tree that provides shade almost all the year round, even when a small amount of water is available.

Acacia tortilis subsp. *raddiana* (Savi) Brenan[37] (Pl. 8)
English: acacia
Arabic: *sayaal*
Distribution: widespread in the north of the Sahara, spreading to Palestine and the north of the Arab peninsula.
Distribution in Egypt: grows throughout the Egyptian deserts. In the Eastern Desert and Sinai, it is restricted to wadis (water collecting channels); while in the Western Desert, it is present in oases and depressions.
Habitat: this tree grows on different types of soil, such as wadi alluvium and sand-covered desert plain, and prefers non-saline soils. It is also found in crevices between rocks and the heavy soils of the Nile Valley. It grows at high altitude, up to 1400 meters in Sinai.

Plant uses: the most useful acacia for firewood and charcoal making. It provides excellent fodder for livestock, and in prolonged rainless periods it is an important source of food for both wild and domestic animals. The wood is hard and good for construction. The spreading root system stabilizes sand. Its gum, bark, and pods are all used in traditional medicine (Boulos 1983). When stems and old branches are injured by insects, they secrete a gum which is used to make candy by Bedouins in Sinai (Danin 1983).

Life form: although it is an evergreen tree, it can shed leaves in dry periods.

Root: the taproot develops at the beginning of the plant's growth and penetrates to a considerable depth seeking water. The surface roots, which absorb the moisture from the soil surface, develop later, after rain. The author was once in the desert with a team of researchers, resting under an acacia tree. No rain had fallen for three months, so we were surprised to hear running water although there were no water sources close to where we were resting. On searching carefully, we found that the sound of running water came from the roots of the acacia, spreading on the soil surface. A small *in situ* experiment showed that the roots of this *Acacia raddiana* contained a large amount of water. A 5-meter piece of the surface root with a diameter of about 1 cm held an average of about 12 ml of water, which was removed by the force of gravity.

Stem: the trees are 7 to 10 meters high, with a distinct trunk, which can reach one meter in diameter in old trees. It is covered by dark gray bark. Both short hooked and long straight spines occur in pairs at the leaf base. Leaves and pods are similar to *A. tortilis* subs. *tortilis*, but glabrous (without hairs). Flowers are spherical, whitish-yellow, and flower at the beginning of spring in the south of its distribution range and late spring in the north. Sometimes the tree flowers twice in a year, depending on rain events.

Crown: young trees have an irregular crown and mature trees have a broad, rounded, umbrella-shaped crown.

Fruits: fruits are pods that are curved or spirally twisted, hairless when mature, containing 8 to 12 seeds. Seeds ripen in late spring.

Regeneration: by seeds.

Availability of propagules: seeds of this acacia are easy to collect during the late spring (April to May) in the wild, because this tree is very common, growing throughout the Egyptian deserts, including Sinai.

Propagation: similar to *Acacia tortilis* as described above, but seeds germinate best at a temperature of around 25°C.

Faidherbia albida (Delile) A. Chev.[38] (Syn. *Acacia albida*) (Pl. 9)
English: white acacia, apple ring acacia
Arabic: *khaaraz* or *haraz*
Distribution: white acacia is native to Africa's dry savannas from Senegal to Sudan. It has penetrated into eastern Africa along the rivers and been recorded in Transvaal and Botswana in southern Africa and Israel, Syria, and Lebanon in Asia.
Distribution in Egypt: this tree has a limited distribution, growing in the Nile Valley near Aswan. Another population has been recorded on the margin of the Nile Valley and the desert near Minya, and a small population of this tree still exists in the south of the Eastern Desert in Wadi Allaqi on the border with Sudan.
Habitat: this tree grows on different soils from heavy silt to light sand. It prefers habitats where underground water is available close to the surface. This trees has the intriguing capability to survive a very long inundation period: trees completely covered by water for more than three years have been recorded in Wadi Allaqi on the shore of Lake Nasser. After inundation, the trees grew quickly, reaching 6.5 meters in height after 4 years and 10 meters after 7 years.

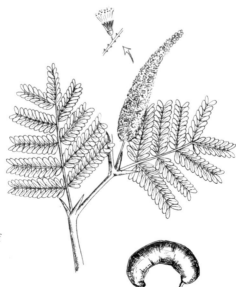

Figure 31: *Faidherbia albida*:
flowering branch, and detail of
flower (top) and fruit (below).
Drawing by Irina Lavrova.

Plant uses: this is an important tree in providing shade, forage, and timber for general construction. Its leaves, small branches, and twisted pods are good fodder for sheep, goats, and cattle. In the driest regions of Africa, the boiled seeds are eaten by humans during famine and widely used in traditional medicine (treatment for coughs, pneumonia, and vomiting are among the best known). It is an invaluable decorative and shade tree for gardens and avenues. Further, its spreading root systems offer excellent protection to the banks of watercourses and improve soil fertility.

Life form: evergreen or deciduous tree. In Sudan, it retains its leaves throughout the dry seasons and sheds them just as the rainy season begins. In this, it differs from other plants, which usually shed leaves in dry periods. However, in Egypt it is evergreen all year round.

Root: it develops a deep taproot and numerous shallow roots.

Stem: it is a large tree, growing as high as 25 meters in areas of Sudan with sufficient water supply. In Egypt, it attains a height of up to 15 meters. The trunk diameter can reach one meter. It has characteristic whitish-gray fissured bark. Bipinnate leaves have 5 to 8 pairs of pinnae and numerous small leaflets (up to 18 pairs). Its white flowers are arranged in elongated spike (inflorescences).

Crown: at the beginning of growth, the young plants spread along the ground and do not form a real crown until they are 4 years old. Mature plants have the characteristic round spreading crown with a diameter of more than 10 meters, which provides intense shade.

Fruits: its thick, swollen, reddish-brown, or even orange, pods are spirally twisted and very distinctive on the crown among the bright green leaves.

Regeneration: from seeds and root suckers. When vegetatively regenerated the trees often grow in a line, following the root suckers.

Availability of propagules: seeds can be collected in the wild from the First Cataract Islands at Aswan with permission from the EEAA.

Propagation: seeds should be released from the pods as soon as they are collected to avoid infection by insects. Because of their hard coats, seeds need pre-treatment before sowing. The most common method is to pour boiling water on seeds, or boil them in water for five minutes, and then leave for one day. Alternatively, the seeds can be put in sulfuric acid for 20 to 30 minutes, followed by washing in running water. The seedlings need about 5 to 6 months in the nursery before being planted out.

Balanites aegyptiaca (L.) Delile[39] (Pl. 10)
English: Egyptian plum, desert date
Arabic: *heglik, laloob*
Family: Zygophyllaceae
Distribution: the Egyptian plum grows in the drier regions of northern, western, and eastern Africa, Palestine, and Arabia. Most commonly found in low-lying semi-arid land, savanna, and desert, it grows also on flood plains.
Distribution in Egypt: at present, it has a limited distribution in Egypt, where it is found in the southern part of the Eastern Desert in water-receiving sites such as wadis (dry riverbeds), the Red Sea Mountains, the Gebel Elba region, and in the Western Desert in Kharga Oasis. Relatively large undisturbed *Balanites* populations occupy the upstream part of Wadi Allaqi close to the Sudanese border.
Habitat: the Egyptian plum can grow in any area of Egypt, other than on the Mediterranean coast and in high mountains. It is adapted to a wide range of soil from sandy to heavy clay and can stand moderately saline soil and short inundation. It is one of the very few trees able to bear fruit during periods of drought and to survive flooding and fire.

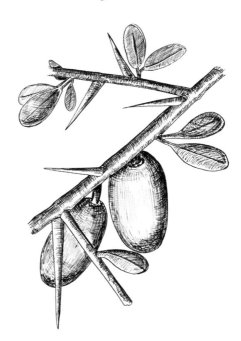

Figure 32: *Balanites aegyptiaca:*
branch with thorns and fruits.
Drawing by Irina Lavrova.

85

Historical records: it was one of the most widely used trees in ancient Egypt. The hard woody stones of its fruit have been found in prehistoric, pharaonic, and Greco-Roman sites. Historical collections, such as those in the Egyptian Agricultural Museum, include fruits and kernels commonly found in pharaonic tombs dating from the Twelfth Dynasty (c. 2000 BCE). The most important pharaonic use of *Balanites* was the extraction of balanos oil from the kernel. This oil was either consumed or used in an unguent or for massage. Hepper (1990) believes that some of the funerary jars found in Tutankhamun's tomb could have been filled with balanos oil. In addition, the fruit pulp was eaten raw or made into cakes and used in the preparation of an alcoholic drink. Its leaves were used as herbs and Egyptian perfumiers used the fruit husks, which they bruised. The wood was used in the manufacture of ships, as recorded from the Cheops boats.

Plant uses: different parts of the *Balanites* tree, which include the fruit, kernel oil, leaves, resin, root, bark, shoots, and seeds, are used to treat a wide range of illnesses and complaints. The reported medicinal roles are extensive and vary from place to place. Local healers develop their own skills, and traditions of medicines have been built up over many generations. For example, the bark of this tree is used by many tribes in East Africa to poison fish and the fruits are used to kill the fresh-water snails that carry schistosomiasis (bilharzia) flukes (Verdcourt and Trump 1969).

Life form: the tree is semi-deciduous, dropping some but not all of its leaves during the dry season. In favorable conditions with sufficient water it stays evergreen all the year. Like most desert trees it grows slowly. It is long-living and inhabitants of Kharga Oasis claim that a few trees growing near the old wells are more than 200 years old.

Root: the *Balanites* tree is relatively deep rooting with a strong taproot that can reach a depth of 15 meters.

Stem: the height of the mature tree ranges from 6 to 12 meters. The young branches are green, turning yellow-brown, with thick rigid thorns. Leaves are alternate compound with two leaflets. Flowers are small and green in clusters.

Crown: the shape of the crown of young trees is irregular and slightly oval while in old trees it is rounded, widely spread, and the diameter can reach 15 meters.

Fruits: the fruit is fleshy with one seed, 3 to 5 cm long, and 2 to 4 cm broad. The tree begins to fruit at about 4 to 6 years and reaches maturity at 10 to 20 years, depending on water availability. Its flowering and fruiting period depends on the local climate. In the most favorable conditions, trees bear fruit and flowers simultaneously. The flowering period in the south of the Eastern Desert is around the end of winter and beginning of spring. Seeds are mature at the end of spring and beginning of summer.

Regeneration: natural regeneration may occur either through seedlings or by root suckers.

Availability of propagules: seeds can be collected in the southern part of the Eastern Desert and in Kharga Oasis at Baris during late spring and early summer. The seeds are also available in local markets in large Egyptian towns and cities.

Propagation: the most common and easiest method of propagating *Balanites* is by seed. Before sowing, the mesocarp (flesh) should be removed by soaking the fruits in water for 24 hours, then stirring them vigorously. The seeds are air dried and extracted from the seed coat. Another good treatment is to feed the fruits to goats and then pick up the uneaten and partly softened seeds which they have not ingested at all. This method has several advantages in that the mesocarp is removed by the goat, which only eats this outer part, and the seed coat is partly softened in the process. The seeds germinate best within a temperature range from 30°C to 35°C in a soil mixture of three parts sand to one part silt. The seeds are sown in plastic packs (three-quarters full). The pointed end of the seed should be uppermost, close to the soil surface. The soil should be kept moist but not over watered.

Seedlings can be planted out when they are 5 to 8 months old. If seedlings are less than five months old they need more care and fewer will survive. It is probable that roots of seedlings will protrude from the plastic bag when they are older than 8 months. The best time for planting is early spring (February to March) or fall (October to November). In the south of Egypt, good results have been obtained in winter as well.

During the first four years, growth seems to be very slow, a four-year-old tree reaching a height of one meter. However, during this time it is developing an intensive root system. In the following years the rate of growth increases considerably, up to 50 cm or even more in height each year. The more water that is added the more rapidly the plant will grow. To facilitate stem growth, pruning of lower branches is recommended when the plant reaches 1.5 meters. Pruning can be used to shape the crown. If *Balanites* is used to form a hedge, special pruning is required to prevent development of the crown and to facilitate growth of the lower branches.

Comments: the Egyptian plum can be planted in any place in a garden, taking into consideration that the tree will become tall and will have a large crown. It can be recommended for providing drainage to certain areas, such as around historical monuments, if the ground water is close to the surface.

Calotropis procera **(Aiton) W.T. Aiton**[40] (Pl. 11)
English: Sodom apple
Arabic: *oshar*
Family: Asclepiadaceae
Distribution: this is a common tree in East Africa and the Sahel, spreading northwards into the Arabian Peninsula and India.
Distribution in Egypt: the plant grows well throughout the country. The largest natural community has been recorded in the southern part of the Red Sea coast.
Habitat: grows in abandoned fields and degraded lands. It does not prefer any special type of soil and can grow well on sandy, heavy silt, or saline soil. It can tolerate high temperature and prolonged drought but may die from over-watering when cultivated.
Plant uses: this plant has various uses, including making ropes from its inner bark.[41] The stem fiber is used for making fishing lines and nets. In many African countries, the plant is used in traditional medicine. Its most valuable component is latex, which is used to treat many human and animal disorders. However it should be noted that this latex is poisonous, and was formerly used as a poison applied to arrows, especially dangerous to the eye. In Africa, some natives used this plant as an insecticide. In his book *Medicinal plants of North Africa* (1983), Loutfy Boulos gives an informative summary of this plant's uses.
Life form: evergreen small tree or shrub.
Root: it has a long taproot.
Stem: the stem is usually about 4 meters in height but it could be as tall as 6 meters when grown in favorable conditions. The stem is softwood covered with thick cork-like bark, which is light brown in color. Leaves are light green, simple, large, and broad, up to 25 cm long. Flowers are white and lightly purple inside, which appear in terminal and axillary clusters (5 to 10 flowers in each).
Crown: it forms a small rounded crown, which gives a little shade.

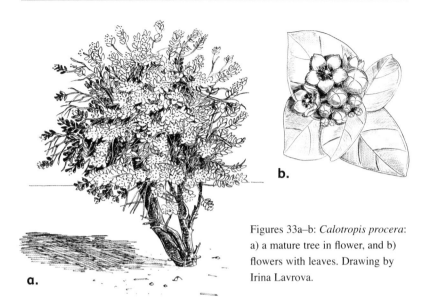

Figures 33a–b: *Calotropis procera*:
a) a mature tree in flower, and b)
flowers with leaves. Drawing by
Irina Lavrova.

Fruits: fruits are large (15 cm across) green in color, rounded and spongy. When mature, the fruit opens and reveals the seeds, which are packed into a compact core and covered by long silky hairs, facilitating their dispersal by wind.

Regeneration: by seed.

Availability of propagules: seeds can be easily collected in abandoned fields, along the roadsides, and on waste ground in or near villages and towns.

Propagation: propagated by seeds, which are easily germinated without treatment and can be planted directly into moist ground. Seedlings will grow rapidly when sufficient watering is applied.

Comments: this plant has very attractive flowers and peculiar spongy fruits giving it an ornamental value. It needs very little tending and can be planted in remote areas, which are not even regularly watered, as soon as the plant matures. *Calotropis* is a suitable plant to be grown in medicinal plant gardens as well as gardens with educational purposes. Care needs to be taken, however, because of the poisonous latex which is exuded by all the plant parts.

Capparis decidua **(Forssk.) Edgew.**[42] (Pl. 12)
English: no recorded name
Arabic: *toundoub, habriga*
Family: Capparaceae
Distribution: widely distributed in the arid regions of the eastern part of the Sahara Desert, tropical East Africa, and North Africa, extending to Arabia and India.
Distribution in Egypt: *Capparis decidua* is widely distributed in Egypt, growing in the Eastern and Western Deserts, the oases of the Western Desert, the Red Sea region, Gebel Elba, Sinai and the marginal zone between the desert and the Nile Valley.
Habitat: it is a very drought-resistant plant, which prefers silt alluvial and gravel soils.
Plant uses: fruits are edible with a high nutritional value, though the slightly bitter skin of the fruit should be removed. The flesh is rich in protein and minerals, and the seeds have a high fat content. Leaves and young branches provide good forage for livestock. Green branches are widely used in traditional medicine in North African countries for treatment of different disorders (Boulos 1983).

Figure 34: *Capparis decidua*: flowering (left) and fruiting branches. Drawing by Magdy El-Gohary.

Life form: its growth form is flexible: it can grow as a deciduous small tree or shrub. When it finds support, it can also grow as a climber.
Root: the plant develops a very extensive root system that obtains moisture from a large volume of soil and penetrates deep into the ground.
Stem: it is a single or multi-stemmed plant when growing as a tree or shrub. When it is climbing, its branches elongate and become vine-like. The bark is greenish and smooth. Very sharp thorns (up to 0.5 cm long), both straight and hooked, densely cover the branches and stem. The small narrow leaves, which occur only on the young sprouts, are soon shed. The charming reddish-pink flowers are especially noticeable on the naked stems.
Fruits: the red, cherry-like fruits are also very attractive.
Regeneration: by seeds.
Availability of propagules: seeds can either be ordered through the Internet or collected in the wild.
Propagation: by seeds and cuttings.

Ficus sycomorus **L.**[43] *(Pl. 13)*
English: sycomore fig, Egyptian sycomore, mulberry fig
Arabic: *gimmeiz*
Family: Moraceae
Distribution: the sycomore fig grows in warm climates, is native to the southern Arabian Peninsula, and extends from north to tropical east Africa.
Distribution in Egypt: this tree is not indigenous, but has been cultivated in Egypt since time immemorial. At present, the sycomore fig trees are scattered, with huge trees still growing in some villages in the southern Nile Valley inviting people to rest in their deep shade. A few large trees can be seen in Aswan and in other towns and cities in the Nile Valley, but not further north than the Cairo area. It also grows in Sinai and the oases of the Western Desert. All plants are cultivated by vegetative propagation.
Habitat: the sycomore fig is found only where there is water not far from the surface. It grows well on heavy silt soil in the Nile Valley. Experiments conducted in Wadi Allaqi have shown that it also can grow in desert wadis on alluvial soil with frequent watering.
Historical records: the sycomore fig has been known in Egypt since the First Dynasty. It had symbolic significance as the tree sacred to Hathor, goddess of the sky and queen of heaven (Wilkinson 1998). It was one of the important trees in ancient Egyptian gardens, planted near habitations

Figure 35: *Ficus sycomorus*: fruiting
branch. Drawing by Irina Lavrova.

to provide fruit and shade, and was one of the main components of temple gardens. The timber of this tree was much used in general woodwork, but especially for constructing wells and sarcophagi, because it resists decay. Its latex (milky plant sap) was used as a remedy for snake and scorpion bites, and for skin diseases. Young branches of sycomore fig have been found in garlands adorning mummies of some Egyptian Pharaohs (Hepper 1990; Boulos 1999–2005, v.4).

Plant uses: the sweet and juicy syconium (fruit of fig trees) is greatly valued for its delicious taste. The wood is light and good for making tools and furniture. Because these trees are not common nowadays, their wood is little used except in villages for fuel and making small items.

Life form: the tree is evergreen but can shed its leaves in the northern part of Egypt in cold winters.

Root: develops extensive root system.

Stem: the tree is up to 20 meters high with large leathery leaves. Old trees have a huge stem that is more than 2 meters in diameter, covered by yellowish-green bark. Leaves are large and leathery. What is popularly known as the fruit is the syconium, which consists of many small male and female flowers arranged inside a hollow fleshy receptacle with an opening on the top through which pollinating insects and wasps enter.

Crown: branches arise from the lower part of trunk, forming a huge compacted rounded crown, which provides good shade.

Fruits: the fruits develop all over the trunk and old branches in large clusters.

Regeneration: the sycomore never produces seed in Egypt and depends on human intervention for its propagation.

Availability of propagules: cuttings can be taken from trees growing in the Nile Valley. Plants are also available in some Cairo nurseries.

Propagation: this tree is easily propagated by cuttings, which should be taken at the end of February and in March. Plant the cuttings in pots or plastic bags filled with garden soil (a mixture of silt and sand) and plant out when good roots develop.

Haloxylon persicum Bunge[44]
English: white saksaul
Arabic: *ghadha*
Family: Chenopodiaceae
Distribution: common in southwest and central Asia.
Distribution in Egypt: in Egypt, *saksaul* is rare, growing only in the north of Sinai.
Habitat: it grows best on sandy soil and can grow on sand dunes up to 40 meters high. Young plants are sensitive to soil salinity while the mature plants can tolerate saline underground water. Danin (1983) observed that plants growing on wadi banks in Sinai are much larger than shrubs growing between wadis.
Plant uses: its most important use is for firewood. In some countries of central Asia, it is extensively planted for this purpose. The foliage provides forage for camels and sheep. It is an excellent sand-fixing plant because of its ability to develop new roots from the stem when covered by sand.
Life form: it is a small tree or tall shrub
Root: it forms an extensive root system and obtains water from a large area of soil.

Stem: saksaul has a stout, rugged stem, which is about three meters high but can grow up to seven meters when irrigation is applied. The stem is covered by light gray bark. Young branches are slender and green. Leaves are very small and scale-like. The flowers are so small that they are difficult to notice.

Crown: the plant is often branched close to the ground forming an irregular, loose crown.

Fruits: numerous fruits with yellowish membranous wings give an attractive appearance to the plant. The seeds are very tiny and dispersed over long distances by the wind.

Regeneration: by seed.

Availability of propagules: seeds can be collected in the wild from the north of Sinai. Because saksaul is widely used for desert planting in arid countries, seeds can be ordered through numerous Internet websites.

Propagation: seeds lose viability in storage and only fresh seeds germinate easily. Seeds can be sown directly into ploughed or dug ground. They can also be sown into pots. Seedlings are planted out when they are one year old and/or have reached a height of 50 cm.

Comments: a plant of the same genus, *Haloxylon salicornicum*, is similar in appearance to white saksaul but is a shrub, about 60 cm high and very common in the Egyptian deserts. It is an attractive shrub, especially in the fruiting stage. By pruning, distinctive forms can be achieved.

Maerua crassifolia Forssk.[45] (Pl. 14)

English: tagart bush

Arabic: *kamoaab, saarh*

Family: Capparaceae

Distribution: this tree grows in north and tropical Africa (including Niger, Mauritania, Morocco, Algeria, Chad, and Egypt) and extends to Palestine, the Arabian Peninsula, Iran, and Pakistan.

Distribution in Egypt: it has a sparse growth but wide distribution, growing in the southern part of the Eastern and Western deserts, Red Sea Hills, Gebel Elba region, and in Sinai.

Habitat: it grows on gravel, silt, rocky soil, and wadi-fill deposits, and tolerates high temperature, prolonged drought, and saline soil.

Historical records: fruits of the tagart bush have been found in burial grounds of the Eleventh Dynasty at Gebelein and may have been growing in the garden of Ineni at Thebes (Wilkinson 1998).

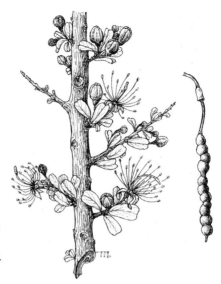

Figure 36: *Maerua crassifolia*:
flowering branch and fruit.
Drawing by Magdy El-Gohary.

Plant uses: the tree is used for landscaping and afforestation. Its flowers are a good source of nectar for honey production. The leaves and fruits are palatable to all animals except horses and donkeys, and the fruits are highly valued by Bedouins for their sweet taste.

Life form: evergreen large shrub or small tree.

Root: its taproot penetrates deep into the soil.

Stem: it is a single or multi-stemmed plant of up to 6 meters in height. The bark is smooth and gray. Small (1 to 2.5 cm) simple leaves grow in clusters on the young twigs. On the top of new twigs, the yellowish-green flowers are arranged in attractive clusters and have a sweet smell.

Crown: it has an umbrella-shaped crown.

Fruits: the cylindrical, pale green fruits are up to 5 cm long.

Regeneration: by seeds.

Availability of propagules: seeds should be collected in the wild in late spring (May to June) when fruits are mature. Ask for assistance from EEAA rangers from the Gebel Elba Protected Area.

Comments: despite little being known about how to propagate this tree from seeds, it has a high ornamental potential and is often recommended for growing in dry areas. This tree is a good candidate for further research on its propagation.

Moringa peregrina (Forssk.) Fiori[46] (Pl. 15)
English: horseradish tree
Arabic: *yasaar, al-baan*
Family: Moringaceae
Distribution: common in northeast Africa, occurs throughout Arabia, and is found as far north as Syria.
Distribution in Egypt: common at high altitudes, growing in Sinai, on the hills along the Red Sea coast, and in the Gebel Elba Mountains.
Habitat: it prefers rocky ground and high altitude, but also can grow on a sandy plain when cultivated.
Historical records: *Moringa* may have been important in ancient times for its oil production. Ben oil extracted from the tree is odorless, yellowish, and sweet-tasting. It was widely used in cosmetics, medicine, and cooking in ancient Egypt. The tomb of Maya, a high official at Memphis in the Eighteenth Dynasty, contained ten jars of ben oil (Manniche 1999). Also it was an important decorative tree growing in Ineni garden (Wilkinson 1998).

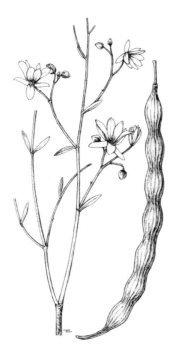

Figure 37: *Moringa peregrina*:
flowering branch and fruit.
Drawing by Magdy El-Gohary.

Plant uses: widely used in traditional medicine, the seed oil being used in perfumery and for encouraging hair growth, while the residues from the oil extraction were used for treatment of various skin ailments.[47] In the southern Arabian Peninsula, the seedling tubers are roasted and eaten. It has a high potential for oil production. Its wood is good for fuel and charcoal production, and is resistant to termites.

Life form: it is a deciduous tree, up to 10 meters in height, which bears leaves only for a short period, usually in early spring, after rain.

Stem: the seedlings are very different from mature plants in that they have large leaves and a large tuber. In the mature tree, the blue-green pinnate leaves become longer (up to 30 cm in length) while the leaflets become narrower. They alternate on the slender branches. The small sweet-scented pink or white flowers are arranged in gorgeous many-flowered panicles.

Crown: the loose, willow-like crown, with thin branches which in most years are leafless, provides little shade.

Fruits: the long (up to 30 cm) narrow fruits are many-seeded and deeply longitudinally ribbed. When ripe they split into three valves revealing whitish-brown seeds that are smooth and ovoid.

Regeneration: by seeds.

Availability of propagules: seeds can be collected in the wild in Sinai and on the hills along the Red Sea coast. Fruits with the seeds inside can also be purchased in the spice and herb markets in any large city.

Propagation: freshly collected seeds germinate well without treatment. The seeds are simply soaked in water and then germinated in Petri-dishes (the rate of germination is about 30 to 40 percent). Scarification can improve the germination of old seeds, which are wrapped in a moist cloth and kept cool in a refrigerator for two or three days. When the radical (primary root) protrudes, the seed should be transferred into a large pot or other container for future growth. Plastic bags can be used for growing the seedlings. When the root system has sufficiently formed, the seedlings are transplanted into the ground.[48]

Olea europaea L. subsp. *europaea* var. *europaea*[49] (Pl. 16)
English: olive
Arabic: *zaitoun*
Family: Oleaceae
Distribution: the olive originated in the Eastern Mediterranean, but is cultivated throughout the world in regions with a Mediterranean climate.

Figure 38: *Olea europaea* subsp. *europaea*: flowering branch (top), and detail of flower (center) and fruiting branch (below). Drawing by Irina Lavrova.

Distribution in Egypt: widely grown, especially in the northern part of Egypt on the Mediterranean coast, in the Nile Delta, and in the oases of the Western Desert.

Habitat: the olive can grow on different types of soils that are poor in nutrients and can tolerate saline soil. It grows well in Egypt on sandy soils. It requires full sun for the best growth, and can tolerate drought, but dies when flooded.

Historical records: it was one of the most important sources of food for people in the Mediterranean region since the Bronze Age. Olive oil was used for food and cooking, as well as in making ointments and for lighting. There are many records of the earliest cultivation of olive in Egypt. When olive trees were first grown in Egypt, the leaves were used for decorative purposes, such as in making bouquets and garlands; olive leaves are present in the garlands of Tutankhamun found in his tomb. Rameses III planted an olive grove near the temple of the sun-god Re at Heliopolis. Reliefs in the Eighteenth Dynasty temple of Aten at al-Amarna in Middle

Egypt show olive branches, and an illustration on an early Dynastic ceremonial slate palette in the Egyptian Antiquities Museum may be of an olive tree. (Manniche 1999; Hepper 1990; Wilkinson 1998).

Plant uses: the olive is one of the most economically important trees for food and the production of high quality oil, and was one of the first trees to become cultivated in the Old World. The wood of olive trees is very strong and lasts well. Inhabitants of Siwa Oasis use it as firewood and to make their doors, windows, clothes chests, and different agricultural tools (Springuel *et al.* 2005). The oil has a characteristic flavor and is very good for health: numerous studies have shown that olive oil reduces cholesterol, lowers blood pressure, inhibits platelet aggregation, and lowers the incidence of breast cancer.[50] In areas with a hot, arid climate, the olive is frequently used as an ornamental courtyard tree.

Life form: it is an evergreen tree or tall shrub that is slow growing and very long living. Some trees in Europe are claimed to be up to 1,000 years old.

Root: it has a well-developed root system.

Stem: it is a single-stemmed tree that sometimes occurs as a multi-stemmed shrub. The linear, leathery leaves are dark green and silvery underneath and new leaves are produced every two years. The white small flowers are arranged into racemes with 15–30 flowers. However, fruits are produced by only 1 or 2 flowers, which are wind pollinated.

Crown: it has a round, spreading crown which provides good shade.

Fruits: fruits are oval with a smooth waxy surface. The color of the immature olive is green, turning to yellow, and then to red, purple or black when mature. The seed is hard and stony-like. The tree starts to bear fruits after 3 to 4 years and reaches its full production 6 to 7 years after planting.

Regeneration: naturally regenerated by seed.

Availability of propagules: it is easy to obtain seedlings and young trees from plant nurseries.

Propagation: the simplest method is vegetative propagation. Even large cuttings root very quickly. Cuttings are usually taken from branches that are 3 to 4 years old. Trees growing from seeds have long juvenile periods.

Comments: the cultivated *Olea europaea* is very similar to wild olives growing in the Mediterranean region. The wild olive is usually named as the subspecies *Olea europaea* subsp. *oleaster* or as the variety *Olea europaea* var. *oleaster*. Wild olives differ from cultivated ones in their smaller fruits and the presence of spines on the lower branches.

Salvadora persica L.[51] (Pl. 17)
English: toothbrush tree, mustard tree
Arabic: *araak, siwaak, miswaak*
Family: Salvadoraceae
Distribution: broad distribution, from the semi-arid and arid lands of central Africa to Arabia, India, and China.
Distribution in Egypt: in Egypt, the toothbrush tree grows mainly along the Red Sea coast, in the Gebel Elba region, the oases of the Western Desert, and in Sinai. A few populations of this plant are scattered in wadis of the Eastern Desert. The numerous fossil remains in wadi channels indicate its much wider distribution in the past. A relatively large population still exists in the upstream part of Wadi Allaqi on the border with Sudan.[52]
Habitats: the toothbrush tree can grow on saline and alkaline soils as well as non-saline sandy or gravelly soil and the rich clay soil of wadi-fill deposits. It tolerates drought well, but usually grows in areas with ground water close to the surface.
Historical record: the wood was used in ancient times for coffins, and its branches and leaves were used in bouquets (Hamdi 2003).

Figure 39: *Salvadora persica*: branch with fruits and flowers and detail (right) of the flowers, appearing with both immature and ripe fruits. Drawing by Irina Lavrova.

Plant uses: one of the most important plants for desert-dwellers. Its leaves and small branches provide good fodder for nomads' livestock as well as for wild animals, such as gazelles, Barbary sheep, and many other herbivores living in the desert. The fleshy fruits are excellent for human consumption with a pleasant tangy but sweet taste, and are sold in local markets in Kenya. However, *araak*'s great claim to fame since ancient times has been its use in cleaning teeth. It is used throughout its distribution area and sold in the market. In Tanzania the young stem is used as a toothbrush, but Egyptians prefer the lower part of the stem close to the roots for this purpose. The plant is very well known throughout the Middle East in traditional medicine. In different countries, people use parts of the plant as remedies for numerous disorders. It is used to treat gonorrhea, swollen spleen, sores, fever, headache, stomach pain, as well as many disorders related to the respiratory tract. Its powdered bark is used in the treatment of snake and scorpion bites.

Life form: this plant has very flexible life forms; it can grow as a small tree when not disturbed, as a shrub, or as a creeper on rocks. It is evergreen and keeps its leaves even during prolonged dry periods.

Root: roots branch extensively from the base of the trunk and are very long, spreading both horizontally and vertically, deeply penetrating the soil.

Stem: it is heavily branched; both stem and branches are whitish, bearing numerous coriaceous (leather-like) leaves. Leaves have a strange smell similar to mustard, hence the alternative name of mustard tree. The greenish-white flowers are very small in a rich terminal panicle. On the same twig the ripe fruits, non-ripe fruits, and buds often appear simultaneously.

Crown: when it grows as a tree, it has a small rounded crown.

Fruits: fruits are small, round berries, light red in color when mature, with an agreeable taste.

Regeneration: by seeds.

Availability of propagules: seeds can be collected in the wild from plants on the Red Sea coast. Plants growing in the southern part of Egypt do not usually produce mature seeds. Cuttings of plants can be obtained from plants growing in the wild as well as from the Botanical Island in Aswan. Take the cuttings from the base of the stem, close to the roots.

Propagation: it is difficult to propagate *Salvadora persica* from seed due to its low seed production. However, if mature seeds are collected, they germinate easily without treatment. Vogt (1995) described the method used in Sudan for propagation as follows: "The ripe fruit should be cleaned of all flesh and afterwards allowed to dry in the sun. It can be sown in the shade without any pre-treatment . . . Germination takes place after about a week." Seedlings should be transplanted from the nursery into the ground when they are 5 to 7 months old.

If seeds are difficult to obtain, vegetative propagation by cutting is recommended by some investigators. Another specialized method of propagation is by tissue culture.

Sesbania sesban (L.) Merr.[53] (Pl. 18)
English: sesban, Egyptian rattle pod
Arabic: *Saisaban*
Family: Leguminosae, subfamily Papilionoideae
Distribution: widely distributed in Africa and Asia from arid to subhumid climates. It has also been introduced in tropical areas of the American continent.
Distribution in Egypt: widely distributed in Egypt wherever water is available: in the Nile Valley, around lakes and pools, in villages and urban gardens. It often grows along roads and irrigation canals.
Habitat: found on a wide variety of soil types from sand to silt, and tolerates alkaline soils. Nodules with nitrogen fixation bacteria are present on its roots in moist soils; these provide essential nitrogen to the soil. Tree can grow at an altitude of up to 2000 meters but cannot withstand frost. It is well adapted to periodic waterlogging and flooding.
Historical records: it was probably cultivated in ancient Egypt,[54] because its branches and leaves were common components of garlands decorating mummies of Pharaohs (Wilkinson 1998).
Plant uses: this tree is a good source of firewood and is used for windbreaks and hedgerows. The wood produces good charcoal and the fiber from the bark can be made into rope. The leaves and pods provide fodder for livestock. The flowers can be eaten as vegetables and the pods can be eaten cooked. Leaves and flowers are used in traditional medicine. A decoction of leaves is used in some African countries for washing animals to prevent tsetse-fly bites.
Life form: a small fast-growing tree, which is short-lived.
Root: this tree has a shallow root system.
Stem: it usually has one main stem but sometimes it is multi-stemmed. It reaches up to 7 meters in height. Leaves are long, pinnate (feather like)

Figure 40: *Sesbania sesban*:
flowering and fruiting branch.
Drawing by Magdy El-Gohary

with many leaflets. Up to 20 yellow flowers similar to those of the garden pea, arranged in a long inflorescence, which is pollinated by insects, mainly bees.

Crown: many side branches develop on the main stem, which give the tree a shrubby appearance. Although the crown is broad, because of the wide angle of the branches, it provides little shade, as the twigs are very slender, and the leaves delicate. In areas that are more humid or those that are under intensive irrigation the tree can develop a compact crown providing good shade.

Fruits: the pod is slender, usually 10 to 20 cm long, containing up to 40 seeds.

Regeneration: by seeds.

Availability of propagules: the seeds are easy to collect, because the tree is widely distributed, and grows close to, or in, urban areas. It often grows in abandoned fields, near water and in the shade of buildings.

Propagation: seeds can germinate without pre-treatment. However, scarification in hot water for just 30 seconds usually improves germination. Direct sowing into the ground is recommended. Sesban can also be rooted from cuttings.

Comments: Sesban is a fast-growing tree, which can attain a height of 3 meters in one year. When grown in the garden it can enrich soil through leaf fall and root nitrogen fixation.

Tamarix aphylla (L.) H.Karst[55] (Pl. 19)

English: tamarisk
Arabic: *athel, athl, atel*
Family: Tamaricaceae
Distribution: native to western Asia and northeast Africa.
Distribution in Egypt: *athel* is one of several species of tamarisk present in Egypt and is widespread. It can be found on the Mediterranean north coast and the southern Red Sea coast. It grows on cultivated land from the Delta throughout the length of the Nile Valley to Aswan, and in the oases of the Western Desert. Numerous fossil remains of *T. aphylla* in the wadis of the Eastern Desert and in small oases in the southern part of the Western Desert indicate its abundance in the past, most probably related to humid historical episodes. In spite of its broad distribution it is difficult to find large populations of mature trees, which may well be because of the loss of natural habitats in the Nile Valley, where every piece of land is cultivated, as well as being cut for its valuable wood.

Habitat: tamarisk has a broad ecological amplitude growing in the riverain, desert, and seashore habitats. It can be planted throughout Egypt; heavy soil is most suitable for its growth, but the plant will also grow on both sandy and saline soils. It can withstand long inundation (about three to four years), for instance when planted on the shores of Lake Nasser, and tolerates hot temperatures as well as frost. The recycling of salts is another interesting ability of this plant. The deep roots absorb underground water, which often contains a high amount of dissolved salts. Absorbed salts accumulate in the leaves, which add to the soil salinity when the leaves fall to the ground. For this reason, only salt-tolerant plants can grow under the canopy of *Tamarix*.

Historical record: tamarisk was a tree sacred to the god Osiris, reflecting the belief expressed in the Coffin Texts that the sky goddess Nut gave birth to Osiris in the Field of Tamarisk (Wilkinson 1998). Another religious

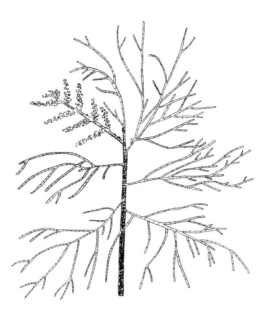

Figure 41: *Tamarix aphylla*: flowering branch. Drawing by Irina Lavrova.

association is with the biblical 'manna' (Exodus 16), believed to be the sweet exudation produced by small scaly insects feeding on tamarisk branches (Hepper 1990).

Plant uses: the wood has been used from the Ancient Egyptian period until today as timber and for making small items of furniture. The wood is dense and used as fuel and for the construction of house turnery. Many old wooden constructions in Kharga Oasis are made from tamarisk wood, which is particularly important for roofing. *T. aphylla* can be used for shade, screening from wind, dust, and blown sand, and for soil stabilization and habitat restoration. It is usually a tree but can be sheared into a dense hedge.

Medicinal values of tamarisk are reported in different publications and the most common uses are summarized by Belal and co-authors[56] as following: tamarisk species "are used as a diuretic, depurative, and sudorific; they are prescribed in Chinese herbal medicine to help measles erupt, also as an emollient for urination, and further to treat alcoholic poisoning; externally, they are used as a wash for skin allergies and as a carminative. Also, the branches and leaves are combined in making a bath or lotion to bathe children with measles."

Life form: it grows as an evergreen tree in suitable habitats in the Nile Valley, but appears as a shrub in the desert wadis.

Root: a long taproot develops, which reaches a depth of 15 to 20 meters, as well as extensive side roots.

Stem: the tree is 12 to 15 meters high. The stem of old trees may attain a diameter of more than one meter. The bark of young trees is smooth, becoming thick and deeply furrowed with age. The leaves are minute and sheath-like. Branches have tiny salt glands, which give a whitish appearance to the crown. The jointed twigs are tough and very slender. The small rose or white flowers that look like little bottlebrushes are abundantly distributed all over the crown.

Crown: when the tree is young, it has irregular conical crowns, which become rounded and spreading when the tree is mature. Their diameter could be more than 10 meters across.

Fruits: the tree produces an enormous number of tiny seeds, which are difficult to germinate because they remain viable for only a few days.

Regeneration: it naturally propagates by seed. However, the seeds need to be soaked in water in order to break the dormancy.

Availability of propagules: mature trees for preparation of cuttings are common throughout Egypt, especially in the Nile Valley.

Propagation: the plant easily propagates from woody cuttings of young branches (about two years old). The best time for preparing the cuttings is in February and March. A young, long twig is selected from the crown of the mature tree and cut into pieces of about 15 to 20 cm long. Cuttings should be grown in a nursery for about 7 to 8 months before planting out. Alternatively, cuttings may be planted directly in the ground. Place the cutting with only 1 to 2 buds above ground and 3 to 5 buds in the soil. The ground should be dug to a depth of not less than 40 cm. Cover cuttings with transparent material, such as glass or plastic sheeting, and water every day. The rate of survival is usually very low at not more than 10 percent of the cuttings. The survival rate is better when cuttings are grown in plastic packs or pots than when they are planted directly into the ground. October and November are the best months for transplanting the cuttings from the nursery into the ground. Cuttings should already have new sprouts and well developed roots. A hole not less than 50 cm in depth should be prepared prior to planting and filled with sand, if the soil is heavy, or with a layer of silt at the bottom of the hole in sandy soil.

Ziziphus spina-christi **(L.) Desf.**[57] (Pl. 20)

English: Christ-thorn
Arabic: the name of the tree is *sidr* and of the fruit *nabq* or *nabaq*.
Family: Rhamnaceae
Distribution: native of North Africa, the Middle East, and south-west Asia.
Distribution in Egypt: mainly a Nile Valley species, growing best in the southern part of Egypt. It is a relict of the pluvial periods in the wadis in the Eastern Desert and Sinai. It is also common in oases of the Western Desert.
Habitat: the Christ-thorn tree has a wide ecological range, growing on heavy soil in the Nile Valley and on alluvial deposits in the desert wadis. It cannot withstand long inundation or soils with high salinity.
Historical record: Christ-thorn is one of the plants described by F. Nigel Hepper (1990) in his book *Pharaoh's Flowers: The Botanical Treasures of Tutankhamun*. He states that it was one of the most important and well-known plants of ancient Egypt, being native to the country and used as food, medicine, and timber. The fruits have been found in pharaonic tombs, and the wood was used to make some of the shrine dowels (joining pegs) in Tutankhamun's tomb. Because of a pair of very sharp unequal thorns growing at the base of each leaf stalk (except in some cultivated trees), it is said to have been used for the crown of thorns of Jesus Christ, hence the name *spina-Christi*, the 'spines of Christ' (el-Hadidi and Boulos 1989).

Figure 42: *Ziziphus spina-christi*: fruiting branch. Drawing by Irina Lavrova.

Plant uses: the outer layer of fruit is edible and sweet when ripe. It is a popular fruit and widely sold in the markets of Upper Egypt. Containing an extremely high proportion of vitamin C, it is an important source of that vitamin for Bedouins living in remote desert areas; they dry the fruits and store them for a long time. Hepper (1990) also mentions that immature fruits are said to be medicinally useful as a laxative and febrifuge. The wood makes excellent firewood and charcoal. Leaves are also given to animals as fodder. In her book *An Ancient Egyptian Herbal*, Lisa Manniche (1999) states that uses of the fruits in pharaonic times included breadmaking, a use that was recorded as having continued in modern Egypt until the beginning of the twentieth century.

Life form: evergreen tree. However, in the cool areas of its distribution, particularly in Sinai, leaves fall in the winter and new leaves appear in the spring. In addition, leaves may also be shed during prolonged dry periods.

Root: it develops a deep taproot and extensive root system, but not as deep as that of other desert trees, particularly acacias.

Stem: the trunk is up to 15 meters in height. The simple leaves are alternatively arranged on the twigs. Spines are present at the base of the leaves. Flowers are greenish-yellow, small, and inconspicuous, appearing mainly in spring and early summer. In the most advantageous conditions, flowering can occur a few times during the year.

Crown: the crown is an irregular oval in young trees and rounded and broad in old trees, providing good shade.

Fruits: fruits are green, turning yellow when ripe, sometimes with a reddish tinge. The largest fruits are up to 3 cm in diameter; when dried, they become dark brown.

Regeneration: easily regenerated by seed.[58]

Availability of propagules: the seeds are best collected from trees growing in the wild. Fruits on sale in markets may have been gathered in the wild, but if they are from a cultivated variety of *Ziziphus* their seeds will grow not well in dry conditions.

Propagation: propagated by seeds and cuttings. The best temperature range for germinating seeds is 20°C to 30°C. For enhanced germination, seeds should be soaked in warm water for 24 hours or the hard coat of the seed can be broken, taking care not to damage the embryo. The latter treatment produces almost 80 percent germination 20 days after sowing. Pre-treatment of seeds with sulfuric acid for 60 minutes also considerably improves the germination. Seeds should be planted to a depth of 1 cm in pots or plastic bags two-thirds filled with soil. The best mixture for seed germination consists of two parts sand to one part silt.

Comments: this is an excellent tree for planting along roads, in gardens and around historical sites. Because of its spines, it can be used for a hedge.

***Dracaena ombet* Kotschy & Peyr.**[59] (Pl. 21)
English: Nubian dragon tree
Arabic: *ombeit*
Family: Dracaenaceae
Distribution: once widespread in East Africa and extending to Saudi Arabia, the dragon tree has declined in the present time.
Distribution in Egypt: it is a threatened tree in Egypt. There is a small population growing in the Gebel Elba Mountains, and another population was recently discovered by Marwan El Azzouni (2003) on Gebel Shindeeb in the Red Sea Hills.
Habitat: This tree grows on hills and mountains on the rock substrata and can survive a prolonged drought period.

Figure 43: *Draceana ombet*: a mature tree.
Drawing by Irina Lavrova.

Plant uses: the leaves of the Nubian dragon tree are used locally for making rope. The stem yields a red resin which is used in traditional medicine, and the mature fruits are edible.

Life form: evergreen tree.

Root: no recorded information.

Stem: the trunk is up to 5 meters in height, repeatedly forked, bearing on the top a rosette of large sword shaped leaves. The delightful but scentless pink flowers are arranged in long inflorescences of about 30–50 cm in length.

Crown: the umbrella-shaped crown provides dappled shade.

Fruits: the small berries (1–1.2 cm diameter) are spherical, bearing one seed inside the flesh.

Regeneration: by seeds.

Availability of propagules: seeds can be collected in the wild in the Gebel Elba Mountains. Ask the EEAA rangers in the Gebel Elba Protected Area for assistance in obtaining the seeds.

Propagation: this tree is difficult to propagate, though Marwan El Azzouni[60] has succeeded in germinating seeds of *Dracaena,* which he collected in the wild in Gebel Elba. It is a slow-growing plant and he still has 4-year-old plants in pots in his nursery in Giza.

Comments: the unusual shape of the Nubian dragon tree with its huge sword-shaped leaves crowded at the top of each fork of the trunk could add to the attraction of your garden. At the same time, by growing this threatened tree, you will be contributing to its protection or even survival in Egypt.

Hyphaene thebaica (L.) Mart.[61] (Pl. 22)

English: Doum

Arabic: *doum*

Family: Palmae

Distribution: widespread in the Sahel from Senegal to Egypt.

Distribution in Egypt: restricted mainly to the southern part of Egypt. It was first described from Thebes, hence the epithet *thebaica.* This palm has been cultivated in Egypt since time immemorial for different purposes, including ornamental.

Habitat: the *doum* tolerates a wide range of soil conditions. It grows in the southern part of the Nile Valley on silty soil and in small oases in the Western Desert on sandy soils. The tree can also grow in wadi beds on wadi-fill deposits. It tolerates high temperature and even fire, as long as the growing tip is well protected.

Figure 44: Drawing after limestone ostracon in the Agricultural Museum depicting two baboons climbing a *doum*-palm tree, from Thebes, about 1440 BCE. Drawing by Nadia Kotb.

Historical records: the *doum* palm has been well recorded, particularly in ancient Egypt, where it was regarded as sacred and as a symbol of male strength. It was also associated with Thoth, the pharaonic god of writing and knowledge, often depicted as a baboon, because baboons often fed on the *doum* fruits (Täckholm and Drar 1950). Many scenes showing baboons on *doum* palms feature in papyrus documents and wall paintings. Well-preserved *doum* fruits were found in Tutankhamun's tomb.

Plant uses: the edible but very hard fruits are particularly enjoyed by children in Egypt. A refreshing cold drink, also called *doum* and made from the crushed fruits, is very popular in Upper Egypt. The timber of the *doum* palm which is strong, compact, and heavy, is used for many purposes: furniture, agriculture, and building. Its leaves have been widely used for basketry, ropes, and similar fibrous items from pharaonic times until the present. Small decorative items are made from the hard seeds, which are sometimes called 'vegetable ivory,' and have been used commercially for making buttons: Täckholm and Drar (1950) note that a factory was once established for this purpose in Suez. Vogt (1995) describes the uses of this palm in African countries where its different parts are intensively used. For example, in Kenya, the powdered fruits are used to make a mild alcoholic drink, while in other countries a wine is made from the palm sap. The fruits and roots are used in traditional medicine.

Life form: evergreen palm

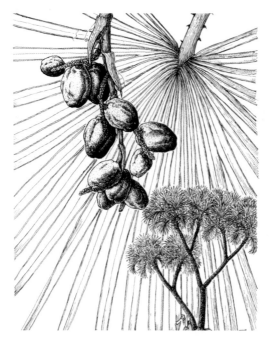

Figure 45: *Hyphaene thebaica*: enlarged leaf in the background; female inflorescences bearing fruits and a mature palm. Drawing by Magdy El-Gohary.

Root: this palm produces a deep principal root and many lateral roots.

Stem: it is a dioecious fan palm with a repeatedly Y-forked stem up to 20 meters in height. When it is cut the wood inside is a light chocolate-brown with black fiber. Leaves are large, leathery, palmate dissected, with a long leaf stalk (of about 1 meter), on the sides of which are many hooks. Flowers are small and yellow and appear from February until April. One male tree will suffice for a great number of females, even situated at a far distance.

Crown: each stem branch terminates with 20 to 30 leaves in a crown.

Fruits: the fruits occur high up among the fan-shaped leaves. Fruits are bumpy, glossy brown, about 4 to 6 cm long and almost as broad. This palm produces fruit without artificial pollination.

Regeneration: by seeds.

Availability of propagules: collect seeds in the wild in Upper Egypt or buy them on the market in almost any large town or city. Because the outer pulp is often used for making the *doum* drink, the cleaned seeds, without pulp, can be bought cheaply from spice and herb shops.

Propagation: by seeds, but this is not easy because of their hardness.

112

Before sowing, remove the outer pulp, soak the seeds in water for 40 days, changing the water every day, and they should germinate well. Plant the seeds in large well-drained containers filled with a mixture of sand and a little silt, kept moist. The plumule protrudes after 3 to 4 months, by when the long primary root will have already developed. Seedlings should be planted out when they are about one year old. Sandy soil is the most suitable, but the plants will also grow in heavy soil. If seeds are sown directly into the ground, they should be regularly watered for a few months, but very few will germinate. Growth of this palm is slow: it starts to produce fruits after 5 to 6 years when the stem is about 1.5 meter high.

Medemia argun (Mart.) Württemb. Ex H.Wendl.[62] (Pl. 23)

English: no recorded name

Arabic: *argoun* palm

Distribution: restricted to the northern part of Sudan.

Distribution in Egypt: one of the rarest species in Egypt. It grows in the small and uninhabited Dungul Oasis in the southern part of Western Desert, where about 35 individuals were recently recorded, among which only three were fruiting. Another small population of this palm possibly still exists in the remote Nakhila Oasis, southwest of Dungul Oasis and very difficult to reach.

Historical records: this fan palm is known to have occurred in ancient Egypt. It was growing in the gardens of Thebes during the Eighteenth Dynasty (Täckholm and Drar 1950). Its fruits have been used since pharaonic times, as findings from Tutankhamun's tomb confirm (Hepper 1990). It is interesting that these fruits were found in Tutankhamun's tomb some thirty years before the tree was rediscovered growing in Egypt in the 1950s.

Plant uses: fruits are very hard and bitter, but they can be eaten if buried in the sand for some time, which gives the endosperm a sweet taste. The leaves are especially important for desert-dwelling Bedouins, who use them to make the mats that cover the *kogra* (shelter).

Life form: evergreen palm.

Root: it develops a deep root similar to the *doum* palm.

Stem: dioecious fan palm, similar in appearance to the *doum* palm but with a non-branched stem up to 10 meters high. Leaves are large, leathery, palmately dissected. The small flowers are arranged in a large, long inflorescence.

Figures 46a–b: *Medemia argun:*
a) a mature palm, and b) its
fruits. Drawing by Irina Lavrova.

Crown: the trunk supports a large, spherical crown of very stiff and strong leaves. The young green leaves on the top of the tree point straight upward, while the old dry leaves droop from the trunk.

Fruits: fruits are about 4 cm long and 3 cm broad, deep purple, with dry, yellow flesh.

Regeneration: by seeds.

Availability of propagules: the seed of *Medemia* is difficult to collect in the wild, because the plant is very rare in Egypt. Seeds can be ordered through the Internet where there are a few websites offering seeds from Sudan.

Propagation: seeds are easy to germinate and need from one to three months to sprout. Before germination, the outer soft layer of the fruit (mesocarp) should be removed and the seeds soaked in water from two to four weeks (change the water every day to prevent fungal growth). Seeds germinate well in pots containing 3 parts sand to 1 part clay. Seedlings should be planted out when they are about 1 year old. The *argoun* palm grows best in Upper Egypt; most probably, it can also grow in the north in sunny places protected from wind.[63]

Phoenix dactylifera L.[64] (Pl. 24)
English: date palm
Arabic: *nakhla al-balah*
Family: Palmae.
Distribution: the date palm is native to northern Africa, southwest Asia, and India and is cultivated extensively in hot, dry regions throughout the world (Microsoft Encarta Reference Library 2004). Some researchers believe that this species of palm is known only in cultivation, although its wild relatives occur from the Canary Islands to eastern India (Täckholm and Drar 1950; Bircher 1995). Others think that it is native to the Near East, the northeastern Sahara, and the north Arabian Desert, of which Egypt is part, and believe that wild individuals occur in Egypt at Sinai, near springs, and in uninhabited oases in the south of the Western Desert (Danin 1983; Zohary and Hopf 1988). It is not clear if these palms were used as the stock for domestication, are the remains of old cultivation, or are escapes from cultivation that have naturalized.
Distribution in Egypt: the most commonly cultivated tree in Egypt, especially in the oases of the Western Desert, the south part of the Nile Valley in Nubia, and in al-Arish on the north Mediterranean coast of Sinai.
Habitat: date palms can grow well on different types of soil from silt to sand, withstand high salinity, and survive both drought and partial inundation. Because the soils in many areas of Egypt are saline, agricultural producers are developing the salt tolerant varieties of this palm for the market. When cultivated, the date palm can be irrigated with brackish water.
Historical records: the date palm is among the earliest cultivated fruit trees. It was already part of the Near East food production in the Chalcolithic period (before 3,500 BCE). The earliest hieroglyph for the date palm appears in the royal tombs of the First Dynasty at Abydos in Upper Egypt, which places it among the oldest recorded words of ancient Egypt (Bircher 1995).[65] Date palm remains have been discovered in numerous Middle and New Kingdom tombs and are displayed in various museums including the Egyptian Agricultural Museum and Egyptian Antiquities Museum in Cairo.

The date palm was an important tree in ancient private and sacred gardens, as can be seen from its depictions and references to it in numerous tombs, temples, and papyrus documents.

Figure 47: *Phoenix dactylifera*: a group of the palm trees. Drawing by Irina Lavrova.

Plant uses: in many parts of northern Africa, Iran, and Arabia, date palms are the main wealth of the people, and dates the chief article of food. They have been cultivated from ancient times, not only for the famous sweet dates, but also for different purposes, such as the construction of furniture from the leaf's midrib. Leaflets were used for thatching, basketry, ropes, sandals, nets, and other small items. The fiber is used as a filter for preparing Bedouin coffee *(gabana)*.

Life form: evergreen palm.

Root: because of their shallow roots, these palms can grow only in places where underground water is close to the surface. Consequently this tree is a good indicator of the ground water that is essential for desert-dwelling people.

Stem: it is a tall palm, growing to about 15–20 meters high, with a slender non-branched rough trunk with distinctive ridges left by the base of old leaves. Palms growing in the wild have many trunks growing from the base of the main stem, while cultivated palms have only one trunk because the lateral ones are removed. The base of the leaves is covered with fiber. The leaves are large, from 2 to 3 meters long, leathery and feathery-shaped. This palm is dioecious (i.e., male and female flowers develop on separate trees) and wind pollinated when growing in the wild. The flowering period is in spring when the strong *khamsin* wind transports the pollen long distances. For good fruit production, artificial pollination is applied, which needs specialized skilled workers, who climb the tall slender stem to reach the flowers at the top.

Crown: only the young leaves at the top of the stem are green while the old dry leaves remain strongly attached to the stem below. In cultivation, the old leaves are cut down annually, leaving only a few young erect leaves, making the crown smaller and giving less shade until these new leaves grow.

Fruits: fruits are ripe in the fall. There are many varieties of cultivated dates, whose fruits vary in size, taste, color etc. However, individuals growing in the wild and not fertilized by man have small fruits (three per ovary) that are not fully developed or sweet, and have small seeds (the stones or pits) inside.

Regeneration: naturally regenerated by seeds.

Availability of propagules: all of the numerous varieties of date palm are available on the market as young plants.

Propagation: the date palm is easily propagated by seed, but cultivators use offspring growing from the lateral buds at the base of trunk (suckers).

Shrubs

Calligonum polygonoides subsp. *comosum* (L'Hér.) Soskov[66]
(Pl. 25)
English: no recorded name
Arabic: *arta*
Family: Polygonaceae
Distribution: common plant in northeast Africa extending to Sinai, Palestine, and Arabia, and eastward to Afghanistan and Pakistan, as far as the Rajputana Desert of western India.
Distribution in Egypt: common in all the Egyptian deserts, especially abundant in the north.

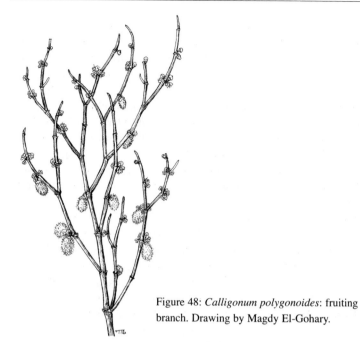

Figure 48: *Calligonum polygonoides*: fruiting branch. Drawing by Magdy El-Gohary.

Habitat: *arta* grows on different soils but prefers the sandy and rocky soils and tolerates saline soil. It is very drought resistant and grows in a temperature range from 0°C to 45°C.

Plant uses: a good sand stabilizer. The plant is grazed by animals in the dry periods, and the woody stems are used for firewood. The small flowers can be eaten in the early spring to enable survival in the harsh desert when no other food source is available. *Arta* is widely used in folk medicine; its tiny leaves are dried, pounded, and used as a remedy for skin ailments, and a decoction of the root is used to treat gum sores.

Life form: a shrub, woody at the base.

Root: it produces a long taproot, which probes into the ground and reaches underground water at a considerable depth.

Stem: the densely branching stem is up to 1.5 meters tall and the plant can be 2.5 meters broad. The young green twigs of this bush spread in different directions resembling a garden sweeping-brush. The leaves are tiny, 1 to 5 mm long, soon deciduous. In early spring, the plant produces silvery-white flowers in long clusters.

Crown: it branches from the stem base and erect branches of different sizes form the irregular crown. Often the base of the plant is covered by sand and only the upper parts of the branches can be seen.

Fruits: the small fruits are red when young, giving a bright appearance to the shrub. Later on, the fruits are covered by soft yellow hairs; the bush is at its most splendid in this stage.

Regeneration: by seed.

Availability of propagules: it is easy to collect the fruits or the plant cuttings in the desert, even close to towns and cities, or seeds can be ordered through the Internet, where many websites advertise them.

Propagation: by seeds and cuttings. Little information is available on growing this plant, but it has been recorded that seeds germinate well in the dark.

Comments: *arta* is a good candidate for landscaping, not only because of its striking appearance but also for its ability to stabilize sand.

Capparis spinosa L.[67] (Pl. 26)

English: caper, caper berry, caper bush

Arabic: *kabbar, lassaf*

Family: Capparaceae

Distribution: throughout the Mediterranean region; spreads northeast to the Black Sea and eastward in Asia to Iran. It is cultivated in many Mediterranean Basin countries and in Iran.

Distribution in Egypt: the Eastern and Western deserts, the oases of the Western Desert and in Sinai.

Habitat: it prefers heavy clay and silt soils and can grow on rocky ground and nutrient-poor gravely soil. It tolerates saline soil, and inhabits rocky cliffs and stony walls near the sea. It requires direct sunlight and tolerates drought.

Historical records: the use of the caper by ancient Greeks was mentioned by Dioscorides, but Pliny stated explicitly that it grew in Egypt (Alkire 1998).

Plant uses: the terminal shoots and semi-mature fruits (the caper berries) are edible when they are pickled. The capers that are familiar as a seasoning or condiment are the flower buds that are cooked or pickled. In Saudi Arabian traditional medicine, the root bark is used as a laxative, diuretic, and analgesic, as well as for the treatment of rheumatism and paralysis. The leaves are used for treating earache, coughs, and diabetes.

Life form: an evergreen shrub, often prostrate on the ground or scrambling on rocks.

Root: develops an extensive root system; the lateral roots are deeply seated into the ground.

Stem: woody at the base with downy young twigs. Sharp spines arise at the base of the leaf. Flowers are large, about 5 cm in size, with pinkish filaments, open at night and early morning, giving a pleasant smell.

Crown: the plant does not form a true crown; it spreads on the ground forming small bushes up to 3 meters wide and 1 meter high.

Fruits: fruits are green, oval, split into segments with the gray seeds embedded in pink flesh. Seeds are ripe in summer.

Regeneration: by seeds.

Availability of propagules: because the caper is cultivated in many countries, its seeds can be ordered through Internet websites. Cuttings can be obtained in the wild. An ornamental dwarf variety is also available.[68]

Figure 49: *Capparis spinosa*: branch bearing flowers, flowering buds, and a fruit. Drawing by Magdy El-Gohary.

Propagation: by seeds and cuttings. Fresh seeds germinate slowly and the germination percentage is low. Dry seeds require initial scarification in hot water followed by soaking in water for 1 day. For enhanced germination, seeds should be wrapped a moist cloth, placed in a sealed glass container and kept cool in a refrigerator for 2–3 months. After refrigeration, soak the seeds again in warm water and leave overnight. Plant the seeds about 1 cm deep in a loose well-drained soil medium. Prepare cuttings in February from the basal portion of the stem. The length of the cuttings should be about 8 cm with 6 to 8 buds. Plant out when it is about 1 year old.

Comments: in Egypt, capers grow best in the north and on the northern coast of the Red Sea.

Leptadenia pyrotechnica (**Forssk**). **Decne.**[69] (Pl. 27)

English: no recorded name

Arabic: many names, the most common in Egypt being *marekh* or *markh*.

Family: Asclepiadaceae

Distribution: broad distribution from the Sahel in Africa to Arabia and Pakistan.

Distribution in Egypt: a common plant in the dry areas of Egypt but is not found in the Mediterranean region.

Habitat: *Leptadenia pyrotechnica* has a wide range of habitats, growing in desert wadis on alluvial soils, in sandy plains and on sand dunes. It can withstand high temperature and prolonged drought.

Plant uses: the young flowers are edible when raw, while the leaves, shoots, and flowers are used to flavor soups. Different parts (sap, seeds, roots, and branches) are used in traditional medicine for treating colds and coughs, urine retention, and to help expel uroliths (Boulos 1983). It is browsed by animals, mainly camels. The plant is used as a windbreak, for stabilizing sand dunes with its extensive root system, for planting along roadsides, and in landscaping.

Life form: leafless shrub, sometimes growing as a small tree.

Root: has very deep, extensively branching root system.

Stem: the shrub is many stemmed and up to 4 meters high. Stems are covered by smooth gray bark. Branches have a characteristic pale green color. The small, velvety flowers, which appear in spring, are yellow-green with a sweet scent.

Figure 50: *Leptadenia pyrotechnica*: fruiting branch with one open fruit containing seeds on the right, and flowers on small branch. Drawing by Magdy El-Gohary.

121

Crown: the whip-like leafless branches form an irregular crown that is almost without shade.

Fruits: fruits are long (6 to 8 cm in length). The green fruits become brown in color when ripe and split open, showing the silky fluff of their seeds, which are then released.

Regeneration: by seed.

Availability of propagules: seeds should be collected in late spring, when the fruits have turned brown, just before they split open.

Propagation: by seeds and cuttings. Seeds do not need treatment and germinate well when they are fresh. Seeds should be sown in plastic bags filled with sandy soil and left in a nursery in direct sunlight. The seedlings are ready for planting out when they are about 4 months old.

Comments: if the garden is established in an area where *Leptadenia* grows close by, you may expect this plant to propagate itself from seeds present in the garden soil.

Nerium oleander L.[70] (Pl. 28)

English: many names, the most common being oleander

Arabic: *difla, ward el himar*

Family: Apocynaceae

Distribution: this plant is native to the Mediterranean region and Southern Asia. It is now cultivated throughout tropical and subtropical regions worldwide.

Distribution in Egypt: grown everywhere in Egypt from the north to the south as an ornamental shrub.

Habitat: the oleander survives drought well and grows on different types of soil from sand to heavy alkaline silt. It can tolerate saline soil and brackish water. The oleander prefers hot climates, yet can grow at a wide range of temperatures and can even withstand short periods of frost. However, it flourishes only in full sun and does not produce flowers if even partly shaded.

Plant uses: widely cultivated as a decorative plant, and grown in gardens for both its scent and beauty, despite the fact that all parts of this plant are poisonous. The effects of its poison have long been known: soldiers in Napoleon's army are believed to have been poisoned by this plant during one of their campaigns.[71] This lesson from history was not learned, and there are still cases in the United States of people being poisoned when using oleander branches as skewers for barbecues.[72] Some Californian

Figure 51: *Nerium oleander*: flowering branch. Drawing by Irina Lavrova.

cities have banned oleander from parks where cookouts are allowed. However, when the toxins are removed, its medicinal value is well recognized in treatment of the heart and circulation problems and the roots are reported to act as a cure for ringworm (Vogt 1995).

Life form: oleander is an evergreen multi-stemmed shrub up to 5 meters high.

Root: it produces very extensive surface roots.

Stem: multiple trunks are covered by smooth greenish-gray bark, the branches grow mostly upright with simple dark green linear leaves, which are arranged opposite one another and covered by thick cuticle. Showy flowers (colored pink, white, yellow, rose, or deep red) are clustered at the end of branches. The flowering season is from March until the end of October in the north, all year round in the south of Egypt.

Crown: it develops a round or triangular flat-topped crown, which provides moderate shade.

Fruits: these are woody and elongated, 8 to 15 cm long, and split open when ripe to release small seeds.

Regeneration: by suckers and seeds.

Availability of propagules: any plant nursery will have a large variety of oleanders.

Propagation: the shrub is easily propagated by cuttings and by suckers.

Comments: requires regular pruning to develop a strong structure. By removing suckers and leaving just one or a few stems, oleander can form an attractive small tree. As all parts of the plant are poisonous, its location in the garden should be carefully selected so as not to be accessible to young children. It should be avoided in areas used for grazing: it is reported that 20 grams of leaves can kill a horse and 1–5 grams can kill a sheep (Vogt 1995). Avoid burning any plant material because the fumes also are toxic. It is recommended for planting in large-scale landscaping, where its abundant, beautiful flowers add color to the area, and along highways and main roads.

Retama raetam (Forssk.) Webb & Berthel[73] (Pl. 30)

English: white broom, white weeping broom
Arabic: *ratam, retem*
Family: Leguminosae; subfamily Papilionoideae
Distribution: North Africa, extending into the East Mediterranean, and into the Negev Desert.
Distribution in Egypt: common in wadis in the north part of the Eastern Desert, the Mediterranean coastal region, and Sinai.
Habitats: it has a broad ecological range, growing in different types of soil, from poor to rich in nutrients, from sandy to heavy; but it needs good drainage. Although it is drought resistant, the shrub grows in areas where rain occurs at least once a year. For best growth and flowering, it needs direct sun.
Plant uses: the plant is highly palatable to goats. Its stem, despite not being very thick, produces a charcoal prized for its high heat. The slender branches are often cut and tied into bundles to support growing vines. In addition, different parts of the plants are used in traditional medicine: the whole plant for making eye wash, the roots in treating diarrhea, and the branches as a febrifuge.
Life form: a perennial shrub, which is leafless for most of the year.
Root: the taproot penetrates deep and numerous lateral roots absorb water from a large volume of soil. The length of roots can reach 15 meters.
Stem: a multi-branching shrub, up to 2 meters high that may reach 6 meters across. Long soft hairs that disappear when the shrub is mature cover young plants. It is gray-green in appearance with slender twigs bearing small leaves, which are shed, together with young branches, during the dry period. After rain new twigs develop. The stem is green and photosynthesizes

during the dry season. The stem of the young plant is covered with soft hairs but it become hairless with age. Flowers are white, 1 to 1.5 cm long, and like those of the garden pea. They appear close to the stem in clusters of 1 to 5. The flowering period is from the end of winter to the beginning of spring (February to March).

Fruits: pods are egg-shaped, from 10 to 15 mm in diameter, containing from 1 to 3 kidney-shaped seeds, which can be yellow, green, or brown in color.

Regeneration: by seeds.

Availability of propagules: seeds can be collected in the wild at the beginning of summer when pods are ripe but still contain their seeds. Many white broom shrubs are found in the desert around Cairo; even in the newly developed areas, the plant still grows along the roads.

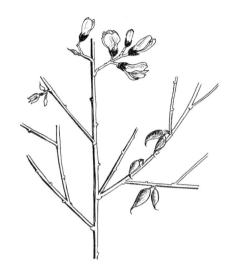

Figure 52: *Retama raetam*: leafless branch simultaneously bearing flowers and fruits. Drawing by Irina Lavrova.

Propagation: seeds can be directly planted in the ground or in pots for propagation in a nursery. Freshly collected seeds germinate easily, without any pre-treatment, but need direct sun for germination. Old seeds are more difficult to germinate, but scratching the seed-coat will produce an increase in the germination rate of some 90 percent. The best time for sowing the seeds is March and April.

Comments: related to white broom is another species from the same genus, *Retama monosperma*, a rare plant in Egypt, growing on the sand dunes of the Mediterranean coast. It is similar in appearance to *Retama raetam*, but has larger flowers. White broom is a potentially dangerous weed if planted outside its native regions, as happened in Australia where it was introduced as an ornamental garden plant, then became widespread and competed with native plants, leading to pasture degradation.

125

Ricinus communis **L.**[74] (Pl. 31)
English: castor oil plant
Arabic: *kharwa*
Family: Euphorbiaceae
Distribution: commonly distributed in East and North Africa and in the Middle East.
Distribution in Egypt: it is cultivated and may be found throughout Egypt growing wild or semi-wild in both rural and urban areas. It grows widely in the Nile Valley and is present on the Mediterranean coast and in Sinai.
Habitat: *kharwa* is a fast growing plant, growing on moist soil close to the river and in abandoned fields. In the desert wadis, its growth is restricted to short periods following rain and the plant produces seeds in a few months. It prefers heavy silt substratum and alluvium deposits but can also inhabit areas with light sandy soil.
Historical records: castor oil has long been used in torches and lamps. Its lighting uses were mentioned by Herodotus and Strabo and its medicinal uses are noted in an Egyptian papyrus text (Hepper 1990). Seeds of the castor oil plant, found in the tombs of the New Kingdom and the Roman period, are displayed in the Egyptian Agricultural Museum.
Plant uses: the best-known use of this plant is the production of oil from its seeds, despite their being mildly poisonous. Castor oil is an important component in soap, printing inks, candles, and many other products. In medicine, its main use is as a purgative. In traditional medicine the leaves are used to treat wounds, and the roots to treat infection by guinea worm (Boulos 1983).
Life form: a tall evergreen shrub, sometimes growing as a small tree when cultivated. In the southern part of the Eastern Desert, the plant grows spontaneously, producing seeds in a few months.
Root: it develops shallow roots, which are widely spread in the upper layer of soil.
Stem: a few stems develop from the base or sometimes it is a single-stemmed plant with a height of up to 6 meters. The stem becomes hollow with age. Leaves are large, palmate, and dark green. Flowers are unisexual on erect inflorescences, the male flowers being borne at the base and the female closer to the apex.
Crown: the young plants form an irregular crown close to the ground. The crown becomes more compact with age, but does give not much shade.

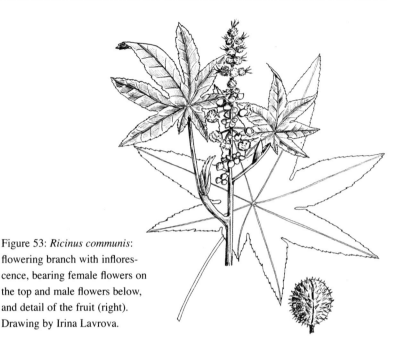

Figure 53: *Ricinus communis*:
flowering branch with inflorescence, bearing female flowers on
the top and male flowers below,
and detail of the fruit (right).
Drawing by Irina Lavrova.

Fruits: the fruit is a spherical capsule with three lobes, each with one seed inside. The fruit is covered with prickles, similar in appearance to a horse chestnut. It is green and turns brown when mature.

Regeneration: by seed.

Availability of propagules: seeds are easy to collect because the plant grows abundantly near towns and villages, along irrigation canals, and in abandoned fields. Collect seeds when the fruits are ripe and have changed color from green to brown.

Propagation: seeds do not need special treatment and germinate well. The growth is fast and the castor oil plant can bear fruits in its first year of growth.

Comments: because of its fast growth, it is an ideal plant to grow in the early stages of your garden, taking care that children should not eat their attractive but mildly poisonous seeds.

Senna alexandrina **Mill.**[75] (Pl. 29)

English: this plant has many names, the most common being senna and Alexandrian senna.

Arabic: *senna mekki, salamekki*

Family: Leguminosae, subfamily Caesalpinioideae

Distribution: native to North Africa, Sinai, Arabia, and India.

Distribution in Egypt: common in the southern part of the Eastern Desert, wadis of the Red Sea Hills, Gebel Elba, Sinai, and in the marginal zone between the Nile Valley and the desert.

Habitat: the best growth is observed on the alluvial soil in the wadi-fill deposits. However, it grows on sandy soil as well. The plant requires high temperatures and tolerates prolonged drought. Senna cannot withstand being waterlogged, nor high salinity.

Historical records: senna is an Arabic name, and the plant was put to medicinal use by the physicians Serapion of Alexandria (200–150 BCE) and Mesue (Yuhanna ibn Masawayh d. 857). Achiarius was the first of the Greeks to notice it (Grieve 1931).

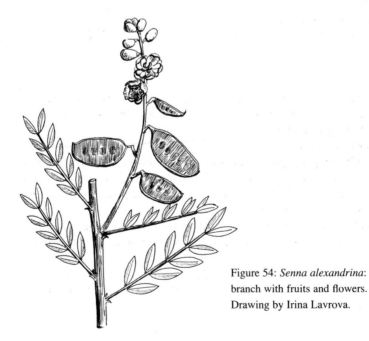

Figure 54: *Senna alexandrina*: branch with fruits and flowers. Drawing by Irina Lavrova.

Plant uses: senna is very valuable for its medicinal compounds. The plant is used in traditional medicine and has a high commercial value. It is best known as a purgative to treat constipation. It is also used in the treatment of influenza, asthma, and nausea (El-Emary and Springuel 1993).

Life form: a small, erect, and fast-growing shrub, producing fruits in the first year of its growth.

Root: it develops a very extensive root system that is widely spread in the ground.

Stem: senna is multi-stemmed, reaching a height of 1–1.5 meter and width of 2 meters. The pale green stems are erect and densely branching at 20 to 30 cm above the ground. The long and spreading smooth branches bear compound leaves with 3 to 7 pairs of elongated grayish-green mucilaginous leaflets, which have a peculiar odor and sweetish taste. The shrub has eye-catching yellow flowers, similar to those of a pea.

Crown: the mature plants form a compact, rounded crown.

Fruits: pods are flat, broadly oblong, slightly curved and contain about 6 seeds. The young pods are green and change to yellow-brown when mature.

Regeneration: by seeds.

Availability of propagules: the fresh seeds of senna can be collected in the wild when ripe. Senna grows most abundantly in the southern part of the Eastern Desert after rain, which happens only once in a few years and can occur at different seasons. As it is difficult to predict when seeds will be ripe. You can buy senna pods in the spice and herb markets, some of which will still contain their seeds. In addition, there are many seed offers on the Internet.

Propagation: fresh seeds germinate without pre-sowing treatment, but the percentage of germination is low because the seed coat is hard. Scarification is recommended to break the outer cover of seeds; either scratch the seeds or put them in hot water and leave to soak for a day.

Solenostemma arghel **(Delile) Hayne**[76] (Pl. 32)

English: no recorded name
Arabic: *argel, hargal*
Family: Asclepiadacea
Distribution: extending from central Africa (Chad, Niger, Sudan) to south of the Mediterranean (Morocco, Algeria, Libya, and Egypt) and Arabia.
Distribution in Egypt: common in the south of the Eastern Desert and also grows in Sinai.

Figures 55a–b: *Solenostemma arghel*: a) flowering branch, and b) fruiting branch. Drawing by Irina Lavrova.

Habitat: *hargal* favors the rocky ground at the edge of the wadi bed and grows in sandy soil as well. It can withstand long drought and high air temperatures.

Plant uses: the leaves and small branches are commonly used in traditional medicine for the treatment of disorders of the liver, kidneys, and respiratory system. It is also used to treat allergies. It possesses purgative properties, which may be due to the latex present in the stems (El-Emary and Springuel 1993). *Hargal* is sold in spice and herb shops. This plant has ornamental value because of its beautiful and fragrant flowers, which attract bees and butterflies.

Life form: evergreen perennial under-shrub.

Root: it develops an extensive root system, which traverses a large volume of soil from which it obtains moisture.

Stem: the plant is up to 1 meter high and as much as 10 meters in diameter when spread on the ground. The young plant has only one stem, but within a few months, as soon as it matures, it develops many branches at the stem base. Its twigs are slender and gray-green. The simple leaves are covered by cuticle, and the inner part of the leaf is whitish-gray. The exquisite white flowers are densely spread on the twigs giving a spectacular appearance to the plant. The flowering period lasts for up to two months at the beginning of spring.

Crown: the young plants have a few erect branches forming a small loose crown. When plants mature and have increased in size the numerous peripheral branches spread on the ground have a hemi-spherical appearance.

Fruits: the purplish-green fruits are very attractive, ovate with a pointed end, about 5 cm in length. When the fruits ripen, they change color to yellow or light brown, split apart and release the numerous seeds, which bear a tuft of hairs on the pointed top. The seeds are blown away from the parent plant by the wind and germinate in favorable habitats.

Availability of propagules: fruits can be collected in the wild in spring (March to April). Collect them before they open, but ensure that they are already mature and their color is yellowish or brownish. Put the fruits in a closed dry place until they open and their seeds appear. These can be stored in a closed dry place. Seeds are available from the Unit of Environmental Studies and Development, South Valley University, Aswan.

Propagation: seeds of *Solenostemma arghel* germinate in a wide temperature range but the best rate of germination occurs at 30° to 35°C. Pre-sowing of seeds with growth stimulators promotes their germination. Survival is better when seeds are germinated in pots or plastic bags rather than sown directly into the open ground. The seedlings can be planted out at the age of 3 to 4 months, in any season except winter. Seeds can also be sown directly into the ground, preferably sandy soil, at the beginning of summer (May to June). Daily watering is required until the first seedlings appear, when it can be reduced to 3 times per week, and to twice a week when the seedlings are 2 months old. The germination is about 30 percent when seeds are sown directly into the ground.

Comments: *Solenostemma arghel* is a vulnerable species, which has a limited distribution in Egypt, being under threat because of its intensive over-exploitation. The largest population of this plant is found in the upstream part of the Wadi Allaqi Biosphere Reserve. *Solenostemma arghel* is cultivated in a demonstration farm in the downstream part of Wadi Allaqi and in the desert garden at South Valley University, Aswan.

Herbs and grasses

Anastatica hierochuntica L.[77] (Pl. 33)

English: rose of Jericho, hand of the Virgin Mary's flower

Arabic: *kaff mariam*

Family: Cruciferae

Distribution: broadly distributed from North Africa to Pakistan.

Distribution in Egypt: grows in all the Egyptian deserts, the wadis of the Red Sea region, Gebel Elba, and Sinai.

Habitat: it grows well after rainy seasons on both gravel and sandy grounds.

Plant uses: according to local beliefs, if a mother during childbirth holds it in her hand or drinks an infusion of its leaves, this will ease her pain.[78]

Life form: it is an annual herb, which dies within one year.

Root: it produces a short tap root with a few lateral roots distributed in the upper soil layer, close to the soil surface.

Stem: this small gray desert plant, which is multi-branched from the base of its stem, drops its small oblong leaves, curls up its branches like a fist when dry, and is rolled across the desert by the wind. After rain, the branches absorb water, open up again, like the palm of a hand (hence its Arabic name of *kaff mariam* which means the palm of Mary) and scatter the seeds.

Fruits: the rose of Jericho bears minute white flowers and small hard fruits, and tiny seeds.

Regeneration: by seed.

Availability of propagules: when seeds ripen in the summer, they can be collected in the wild, in the desert just outside Cairo, as well as throughout the northern part of the Egyptian deserts. Seeds are inside the dry plants when they are sold in the market. However, if seeds stay very long inside the plant they can lose viability and will not germinate.

Propagation: only fresh seeds can germinate without any treatment. Seeds should be sown in February in the south of Egypt and March to April in the north (Hegazy, personal communication 2005).

Comments: *kaff mariam* is frequently sold in spice and herb shops as a novelty, where a fully opened plant is displayed in a bowl of water alongside the curled up dried plants.

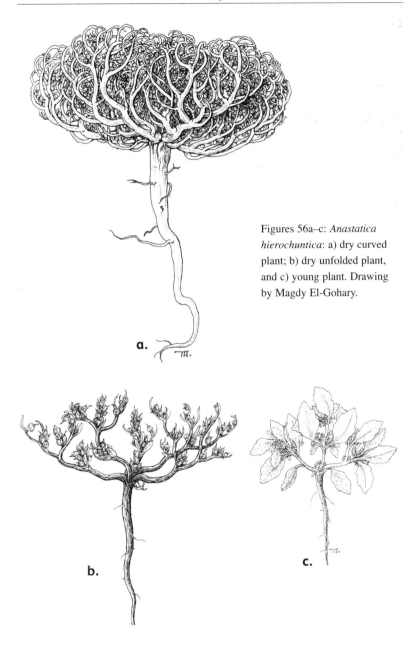

Figures 56a–c: *Anastatica hierochuntica*: a) dry curved plant; b) dry unfolded plant, and c) young plant. Drawing by Magdy El-Gohary.

a.

b.

c.

Datura innoxia Mill.[79] (Pl. 34)

English: downy thorn apple, angel's trumpet

Arabic: *tatura*, *datura*

Family: Solanaceae

Distribution: native to Central America from where it has become distributed throughout warm and tropical climates worldwide.

Distribution in Egypt: widely distributed from north to south in the Nile Valley and is also found on the Mediterranean coast.

Habitat: it grows on different soils, from sand to silt, and on rocky ground in the transition zone between the Nile Valley and the desert. The downy thorn apple is common in abandoned fields, alongside roads and canals, and in waste areas. It is tolerant of short periods of drought and high air temperatures.

Plant uses: the downy thorn apple is widely cultivated as an ornamental plant throughout the world from tropical Africa to temperate Canadian lands. Its medicinal value has a long history and most probably was the reason for its introduction from Central America to many other countries including Egypt, where it has long been naturalized. Although it is a poisonous plant, its leaves are used as an intoxicant and a hallucinogen in Saudi Arabia.

Life form: annual herb, appearing as a shrub with a height of up to 70 cm.

Figure 57: *Datura innoxia*: plant branch with single flower at top and an immature fruit. Drawing by Irina Lavrova.

Root: the lateral roots are widely spread near the soil surface.
Stem: it has a few stems beginning from the base of the plant. Leaves are
large, oval, and whitish-green with a wedge-shaped base. Its impressive
large flowers are up to 15 cm in length, white and trumpet-shaped. It flowers in the spring.
Fruits: it produces a peculiar walnut-sized fruit, covered with spines.
Regeneration: by seed.
Availability of propagules: because *Datura* grows in Egypt wherever
water is available, the seeds can be collected in many places just outside
towns and cities. On the edges of cultivated fields in the Nile Delta, this
plant is conspicuous with its attractive large white flowers. It is very common at al-Arish, Sinai, in holiday resorts near the seashore. The best time
for seed collection is the middle of summer. Seeds can readily be ordered
through many websites on the Internet.
Propagation: the freshly collected seeds germinate without pre-treatment
but the germination percentage is low. To break the seed dormancy and
improve the germination of old seeds, pre-sowing treatment by soaking in
hot water is recommended.
Comments: when planting in a garden, care should be taken to plant it out
of the reach of young children, as all the parts of this gorgeous-looking
plant are poisonous.

Arundo donax L.[80] (Pl. 35)
English: giant reed, Persian reed
Arabic: *ghaab baladi, ghaab rumi*
Family: Gramineae
Distribution: originated in the Mediterranean region from where it has
spread, partly through cultivation and then naturalization, to many areas of
the world with tropical and subtropical climates.
Distribution in Egypt: the giant reed grows in the Nile Delta and Valley,
and on the Mediterranean coast. There is strong evidence that this grass
was widely cultivated in Egypt in ancient times. It was probably introduced into ancient Egypt from Syria.
Habitat: this grass prefers slightly alkaline, heavy, but well aerated moist
soil. It can also grow on sandy soil when ground water is close to the surface. Young plants are very sensitive to drought, but when the plant is
mature it can tolerate long periods of drought because of its well-developed root system. The giant reed is fast growing in favorable habitats.

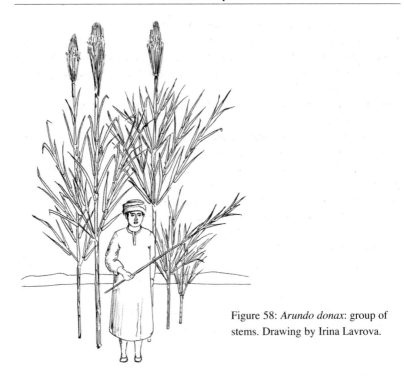

Figure 58: *Arundo donax*: group of stems. Drawing by Irina Lavrova.

Historical records: this is an intriguing grass, having been cultivated since prehistoric times. The earliest archaeological record of the giant reed is from the Neolithic period, when it was used to line underground pits for the storage of grain. The remains of *Arungo donax* have been found in pharaonic tombs; the leaves were most probably used to wrap the mummies. The culms (hollow grass stems) were used by ancient Greeks to make the arrows and pens. The reed has even had an effect on the development of musical instruments; the original primitive pipe organ, which dates back to 5000 BCE, was made from this giant reed grass.[81]

Plant uses: this grass has numerous uses even today. It is very common in Egypt and used for fencing, sheltering crops, and supporting flowering plants and grapevines. It is also used to make baskets and mats, and the *goza*, a simplified water pipe for smoking tobacco. It is cultivated for ornamental purposes in many parts of the world with suitable climates, including the United States of America.

Life form: stout tall perennial grass.

Root: this grass develops coarse thickly branched rhizomes and extensive roots, which densely penetrate into the ground.

Stem: *Arundo* is a reed-like grass, usually 3 to 4 meters in height, reaching 8 meters in favorable habitats. Culms (hollow grass stems), 1–4 cm in diameter, grow in large clumps. Leaves are numerous, elongated, 5–8 cm broad at the base, which has hairy tufts. The small flowers are in a large terminal panicle up to 70 cm long, which is symmetrical and softly feathered.

Regeneration: by seeds and rhizomes.

Availability of propagules: it is easy to collect the rhizomes along the irrigation canals, on roadsides, and close to lakes and pools.

Propagation: propagated by planting out cuttings from the rhizomes directly into the ground in places selected for their growth. *Arundo* is easy to establish and requires minimal care.

Cymbopogon schoenanthus **subsp.** *proximus* **(Hochst. ex A. Rich)**
Maire & Weiller (Pl. 36)

Syn. *Cymbopogon proximus*[82]

English: no recorded name

Arabic: *Halfa barr*

Family: Gramineae

Distribution: dry regions of north-east Africa in Sudan and Eritrea, the northern part of Nigeria and Socotra Island in Yemen.

Distribution in Egypt: *halfa barr* has a very limited distribution in Egypt, growing in the far south of the Eastern Desert on the border with Sudan. It is threatened in Egypt, most probably because of over-exploitation in the past.

Habitat: this grass grows well on the alluvial deposits in desert wadis, in rocky habitats, and on sandy soil. It likes high temperatures and tolerates prolonged periods of drought.

Historical records: it seems that *halfa barr* was known in ancient Egypt and was one of the ingredients to make the famous *kyphi*, a scent free from oil and fat (Manniche 1999).

Plant uses: *halfa barr* is famous for its medicinal properties. It is used intensively in indigenous medicine as a diuretic, painkiller for colic, and antipyretic. It is used pharmaceutically in preparing the drug Proximol. *Halfa barr* is a healthy and refreshing hot drink, especially popular in Upper Egypt.

Life form: this is a perennial aromatic grass.
Root: it has fibrous and shallow roots.
Stem: it is very densely tufted, its tufts reaching a height of up to 1 meter and diameter of 60 cm. The grass has narrow leaves and a reddish panicle.
Regeneration: by seed.
Availability of propagules: these cannot be collected in the wild, because of the plant's rarity in Egypt and its presence only in a Protected Area. Propagules, both seeds and parts of the plant, are available from the Unit of Environmental Studies and Development, South Valley University, Aswan.
Propagation: *halfa barr* can grow from seeds, but is best propagated by root cuttings. The seeds are minute and difficult to germinate because of their long dormancy period; they need to be in the soil for at least eight months before they will germinate. However, once established, *halfa barr* will freely self-propagate to the extent that it will grow everywhere in the surrounding area where moisture is available, even as a weed.[83]
Comments: *halfa barr* should be clearly distinguished from the dangerous invasive weed *Imperata cylindrica*, which has a similar name, *halfa*, and has spread everywhere in Egypt, becoming almost impossible to eradicate from cultivated fields, orchards, and gardens.

Figure 59: *Cymbopogon schoenanthus:* part of plant with seeds. Drawing by Irina Lavrova.

Afterword

Egypt, being a desert country, is not rich floristically, but each of the two thousand or so plants that grow in the wild[84] has its own beauty. The plants described in this book represent less than two percent of all Egyptian plants and grow mainly in the Eastern and Western Deserts of Egypt. Many other plants from the mountain areas of Sinai and Gebel Elba are still waiting for further research and later publication. Yet I hope this book has opened a small window onto the unexplored potential of indigenous desert plants for ornamental purposes.

There are many other native plants which may be used in gardening. Here follows a short account of some perennial plants (mainly from Sinai and Gebel Elba) which the author believes to have potential as elements for desert landscape gardening, though they have not been described in the body of this book.

Many plants from the Malvaceae family have exceptionally beautiful flowers, particularly *Abutilon pannosum*[85] and *Pavonia hirsuta*, perennials with purple-centered yellow flowers growing in the wadis of the Eastern Desert. Perennial herbs from Sinai include *Alcea striata* with creamy-white flowers, *Alcea apterocarpa* with white, yellow, pink, or violet flowers, and *Alcea rosea*[86] with beautiful large and delicate flowers of various hues. In Gebel Elba, on rocky hillsides, the shrub *Hibiscus vitifolius* produces large yellow flowers with a maroon centre.

Among the few plants of the poppy family (Papaveraceae) found in Egypt, the species of *Glaucium* genus growing in Sinai are very attractive, with large bright flowers. In particular, *G. grandiflorum*, the horned poppy, has already been domesticated for ornamental use, because of its spectacular brilliant orange silky flowers with a dark spot on each petal.

There are a few plants from the family Rosaceae in Egypt, including *Rosa arabica*, a very rare shrub endemic in Sinai, growing on high mountains with beautiful fragile pink flowers. There are two *Crataegus* shrubs (*C. azarolus* and *C. sinaica*), both of which are rare, growing on the mountains in Sinai. The former can grow as a small tree. Both are deciduous, shedding leaves in winter, while in spring intensive white blooms cover the shrubs. Fruits are red when ripe and remain on the plants most of the year, giving a spectacular appearance, especially in winter on the bare branches.

Among plants of the Leguminosae family, a very striking yellow-flowered tree is *Delonix elata*,[87] which grows on the stony hillsides of Gebel Elba and is a wild relative of the widely cultivated ornamental tree *Delonix regia*, popularly known as the flamboyant or flame tree, with red or orange and purple-red flowers. The evergreen small tree *Ceratonia siliqua,* very rare in the wild and growing only in Sinai, is also a good candidate for the desert garden.

The family Oleaceae is represented in Egypt with only two genera: *Olea* and *Jasminum*. The olive tree, which is widely cultivated in Egypt, is described earlier in this book while another tree from the same genus, *Olea europaea* subsp. *cuspidata*, grows wild on the slopes of the Gebel Elba mountain group. The genus *Jasminum* is well known for its sweet-scented ornamental flowers. Two species of this genus *Jasminum grandiflorum* subsp. *floribundum* and *J. fluminense* subsp. *gratissimum* both scramble over the Gebel Elba Mountains at high altitude. *Lantana viburnoides* (F. Verbenaceae), also from the Gebel Elba region, has pink or white flowers from the same genus as *L. camara*, a well-known ornamental shrub that is now naturalized in Egypt.

Many convolvulus annuals or perennials (family Convolvulaceae) have very attractive flowers. The handsome perennials *Convolvulus hystrix* and *C. lanatus* are low shrubs with distinctive flowers (blue in the former and pinkish-white in the latter); both are common throughout Egyptian deserts. *Convolvulus dorycnium* and *C. oleifolius* are small shrubs with pink flowers growing on the Mediterranean coast. In Sinai the liana-like *C. scammonia*, with large yellow flowers grows on the hillsides, and *Ipomoea pes-caprae*, a creeping perennial with pink or reddish-purple flowers, grows higher in the mountains.

The stem succulents have outstanding ornamental value, such as the cactus-like *Euphorbia polyacantha* (F. Euphorbiaceae) and *Caralluma acutangula*[88] from the family Asclepiadaceae (both plants are from Gebel Elba mountain region). Other *Euphorbia* species that can contribute in landscaping are *E. dendroides,* a woody shrub with Y-shaped branching, from the west of the Mediterranean coast, found near Sallum and Mersa Matruh, and the succulent *E. consobrina* growing on the slopes of the Gebel Elba Mountains and the Red Sea Hills.

Stem succulents of the family Chenopodiacee, *Haloxylon salicornicum* and *Anabasis articulata,* are common desert plants with eye-catching and delicate fruits of different shades, ranging from yellowish-green to rose-colored, both of which make attractive bouquets.

Species of *Pistacia* and *Rhus* are the only two genera in the family Anacardiaceae in Egypt, and are trees or shrubs growing on the mountains of Gebel Elba or Sinai. *Pistacia khinjuk* and *Pistacia atlantica* are deciduous trees that grow at a high altitude in Sinai. In the fall before the leaves fall, they become bright red. Another interesting tree that grows in the hills of northern Sinai is *Juniperus phoenicea* (family Cupressaceae), the common juniper of the Mediterranean region, which is very rare in Egypt. Plants that have been already domesticated and widely used for hedges in landscaping include *Dodonaea viscosa* from the family Sapindaceae, which relatively few people have seen in the wild, growing in Gebel Elba Mountains.

There are many other native Egyptian plants which have the potential to be grown for decorative purposes. This book is just an attempt to increase interest in this new approach to gardening in Egypt.

141

Notes

1. Marie-Luise Gothein, *A History of Garden Art*; this comprehensive history of garden design by Gothein (1863-1931) was published in German in 1913 and re-published in English in 1928. This edition has been edited, revised, and encoded for copyright protection ©Tom Turner 2000 <http://www.gardenvisit.com/got/index.htm>.

2. In this book, the Latin names of plants are given following Vivi Täckholm, *Students' Flora of Egypt* (1974) and Loutfy Boulos, *Flora of Egypt*, vols. I–IV (1999–2005). The transliterated Arabic names have been taken from different sources.

3. The term 'ephemeral,' as used here, means that run-off water, which forms a temporary stream, may occur only once in many years. In addition, the stream is mainly localized and water runs into only one of the wadi's tributaries but not into a neighboring tributary. On some occasions, the run-off water does not even reach the main wadi channel. On very rare occasions, the run-off water reaches the River Nile.

4. John Ball (1912) refers to "Linant's experience about 1830, when he recorded that the torrent from the Wadi Allaqi into the Nile was so great as to prevent his *dahabia* sailing up the river past the point of influx, even with good wind and all sails set."

5. In his book *Deserting the Desert*, Knut Krzywinski (2001) refers to the old tradition of *ewak* in the Eastern Desert, which goes back to pharaonic times, illustrating this with a picture from a New Kingdom tomb at Thebes where men cut branches, most probably acacia trees, with an axe, while goats gather to browse the cut branches on the ground.

6. Sampsell 2003.

7. The British administrator C. Dalrymple Belgrave was stationed in Siwa 1920–21, in command of a section of the Frontier Districts Administration Camel Corps. He wrote a comprehensive account of his experiences, together with a survey of the history and culture of the oasis, remarkably detailed and observant, providing invaluable and comprehensive documentation. Dalrymple Belgrave 1922, intro. Reginald Wingate.

8. Date wine is referred to in ancient texts from the Second Dynasty (Hepper 1990).

9. William Baker, Head of Palm Research at the Herbarium, Royal Botanic Gardens, Kew, went to Dungul Oasis to study the current conditions of *Medemia argun*. He was accompanied by Haytham Ibrahim, who invited him on this trip, and other staff of the Unit of Environmental Studies and Development at South Valley University, Aswan.

10. Two mature individuals of the extremely rare *Acacia arabica* are growing in the grounds of the Agricultural Museum in Doqqi, Cairo, and the Orman Garden in Giza respectively, where they are cultivated at least 50 years ago. These trees produce many seeds and are surrounded by small seedlings.

11. Wadi Allaqi, the largest wadi in the south of Egypt's Eastern Desert, was declared a conservation area in 1989, and was designated a biosphere reserve in 1993 within the UNESCO Man and Biosphere Programme (MAB). The Desert Field Station and the Conservation Centre in Wadi Allaqi provide research facilities for local and overseas researchers working in the Wadi Allaqi Biosphere Reserve. For information on Wadi Allaqi, see Belal and Springuel 1997.

12. A striking aphorism, included in the display of ancient plants at the Egyptian Agricultural Museum in Doqqi, Cairo, says: "Plant any tree at the end, but you should begin with planting a sycomore tree" (Ankh-Shashenqi, fifth century BCE). A variant spelling of this tree's name is sycomore fig.

13. References used: Hepper 1990; Wilkinson 1998 and Manniche 1999.

14. The reproductive biology of this tree is fascinating and merits a brief description. The tree bears its fruit on small leafless branches that arise directly from the trunk. The fruit has three types of flower: male, female, and the gall flowers, which are modified female flowers. All flowers are enclosed in fleshy receptacles (the flower-bearing part of the plant) with only one small opening or 'eye,' a type of fruit known as syconium or fig. Because the flowers are enclosed inside the fleshy walls of the fig, the remarkable fertilization depends on interaction with a wasp. The female wasps enter through the 'eye,' lay their eggs on the gall flowers, *and then die*, whereupon the opening is closed. Both male and female wasps are hatched from the eggs. The male wasps emerge first and then fertilize the female wasps, which are still in the gall flower. The males then try to leave the fig by eating through its fleshy walls. However, as soon as they make a hole, the sunlight penetrates the dark fig enclosure, killing the male wasps, which are blind and wingless. The female wasps, which have become well developed, emerge easily from the gall flowers a day later, through the hole made by the male wasps. They carry on their bodies the pollen

to fertilize another fig and the new cycle begins. Each species of fig has its own wasp fertilizer, and sadly the wasps which formerly fertilized the sycomore figs have long disappeared from Egypt. Without fertilization, the fruit falls to the ground and rots. At present, the propagation of this intriguing tree depends totally on human intervention (Miller and Morris 1988).

15. Gothein 1913.
16. For uses of plants growing in Wadi Allaqi see Belal and Springuel 1996.
17. Contact Dina Aly (e-mail: rafikha@tedata.net.org) to obtain seedlings and saplings of *Balanites aegyptiaca, Moringa peregrina, Ziziphus spina-christi, Delonix elata, Capparis* spp., *Leptadenia pyrotechnica, Retama raetam*, several indigenous acacia species and many other desert plants. You can also arrange to visit the garden and/or to consult Dina Aly.
18. Egyptian Environmental Affairs Agency (EEAA) represents the executive arm of the Ministry of State for Environmental Affairs. The Natural Protection Central Department within EEAA is responsible for all Protected Areas in Egypt. Its website is <http://www.eeaa.gov.eg/english/main/protectorates.asp>.
19. The contact persons are Professor Ahmed Belal, the Founder and Director of the Unit of Environmental Studies and Development at South Valley University (e-mail: abelal39@yahoo.com) and the author of this book.
20. Professor Ahmed Hegazy in the Botany Department of Cairo University, (e-mail: akhegazy2202@hotmail.com) is experienced in the propagation of desert plants. He can advise, as well, on the collection of seeds.
21. This information is given by Marwan El Azzouni, an Egyptian businessman who lives in Giza and has a special interest in growing exotic tropical plants and native desert plants, notably *Draceana ombet* and *Caralluma acutangula*, both of which are from the Gebel Elba Region.
22. Adventitious roots develop in unusual positions, for example as a root growing downwards from the plant's branch, leaves, or trunk.
23. Hartmann *et al.* (1990) describe the different methods and techniques in *Plant Propagation, Principles and Practices.*
24. A warning about using drip irrigation for drought-tolerant plants is provided by Las Pilitas, a Californian nursery specializing in Californian native plants, website: <http://www.laspilitas.com/drip.htm>. They advise that under drip irrigation, the lifespan of these plants becomes short; they are unhealthy and less resistant to disease.
25. David Bainbridge, a researcher from Alliant International University, San Diego, gives a detailed explanation of the buried clay pot irrigation technique in his paper: Bainbridge, D.A. 2001, "Buried clay pot irrigation: a little

known but very efficient traditional method of irrigation." *Agricultural Water Management* 48: 79–88.

26. Some plants described in this section can grow into trees under optimal conditions, but under harsh conditions or through human activities (repeated cutting) they acquire a bush form.

27. Shaheen 1995.

28. A spine is a hardened, modified stipule with a sharp point which may be short or long, straight or curved. A prickle is a hardened epidermal outgrowth, also with a sharp point which is short and curved.

29. References used: Täckholm 1974; Shaheen 1995; Springuel and Mekki 1994.

30. References used: Sahni 1968; Vogt 1995; Shaheen 1995.

31. References used: Täckholm 1974; Sahni 1968; Shaheen 1995; Vogt 1995.

32. References used: Sahni 1968; Manniche 1989; Hepper 1990; Shaheen 1995; Vogt 1995.

33. References used: Shaheen 1995; Smit 1999; Boulos 1999–2005, v. 3.

34. Dina Aly has a nursery in her desert garden in the Oraby district near Cairo, where she grows indigenous plants including *Acacia pachyceras:* see note 17.

35. References used: Advisory Committee on Technology Innovation 1980; Shaheen 1995; Vogt 1995.

36. References used: National Academy of Sciences 1979; Advisory Committee on Technology Innovation 1980; Shaheen 1995; Boulos 1999–2005, v. 3.

37. References used: Sahni 1968; Advisory Committee on Technology Innovation 1980; Springuel and Mekki 1994; Shaheen 1995; Boulos 1999–2005, v. 3.

38. References used: Sahni 1968; National Academy of Sciences 1979; Vogt 1995; Shaheen 1995.

39. References used: Sahni 1968; Hall 1992; Vogt 1995.

40. References used: Verdcourt and Trump 1969; Vincett 1977; Vogt 1995; Zoghet and Alsheikh 1999.

41. Vogt (1995) in his book *Common Trees and Shrubs of Dryland Sudan* writes: "In Sudan rope was made from this species by the prison department of Port Sudan on a commercial basis in the 1950s." It was cultivated for the same purpose, in Latin America.

42. References used: Vogt 1995; Guinand and Lemessa 2001.

43. References used: Miller and Morris 1988; el-Hadidi and Boulos 1989; Hepper 1990.

44. References used: Advisory Committee on Technology Innovation 1980; Danin 1983; Zoghet and Alsheikh 1999.

45. References used: Sahni 1968; Zoghet and Alsheikh 1999.

46. References used: Miller and Morris 1988; Hepper 1990; Boulos 1999–2005, v. 3.
47. For more details on plant uses see Miller and Morris 1988.
48. Hegazy, personal communication, 2005.
49. References used: Zohary and Hopf 1988; Boulos 1999–2005, v. 2.
50. Francis 1998.
51. References used: Miller and Morris 1988; Vogt 1995.
52. Intensive use of *araak* through the millennia has probably affected its growth form. The plant commonly spreads on the ground and accumulates soft material brought by wind and water, forming phytogenic hillocks. Severe aridity combined with over-exploitation and the inappropriate practice of cutting lower parts of the stem (as opposed to cutting higher up) are the main reasons that this plant is threatened in Egypt.
53. Vogt 1995; Boulos 1999–2005, v. 3; Suttie 2005; Evans 1994.
54. Fernandes 2003.
55. References used: Sahni 1968; Advisory Committee on Technology Innovation 1980; Vogt 1995.
56. Belal, Leith, Solway, and Springuel 1988.
57. References used: Sahni 1968; Advisory Committee on Technology Innovation 1980; Vogt 1995.
58. Christ-thorn trees are common along roads and in public gardens throughout Egypt, and many have grown from seeds thrown away while the fruits were being eaten.
59. References used: El Azzouni, M. 2003; Boulos 1999–2005, v. 4.
60. Marwan El Azzouni, personal communication, 2005.
61. References used: Sahni 1968; Täckholm and Drar 1950; Vogt 1995.
62. References used: Täckholm and Drar 1950; Hepper 1990; Boulos 1999–2005, v. 4.
63. Young individuals of *argoun* palm grow in Dina Aly's garden near Cairo.
64. References used: Täckholm and Drar 1950; Corner 1966; Bircher 1995.
65. Bircher (1995) gives the history of date palms and includes a long chapter dealing with date palms in pharaonic Egypt.
66. References used: Vincett, 1977; Zoghet and Alsheikh 1999; The Aircav® Survival-Appendix B, Edible and medicinal plants <http://www.aircav.com/survival/appb/asappbtoc.html>.
67. References used: Alkire 1998; Zoghet and Alsheikh 1999; *Mediterranean climate gardening throughout the world* www. Mediterranegardensociety.org/plants/Capparis.spinosa
68. Onlineshop, 2005. ©Daniel Rühlemann <www.ruehlemanns.de>.
69. References used: Vincett 1977; Vogt 1995; Zoghet and Alsheikh 1999.

70. References used: Giman and Watson 1994; Vogt 1995.
71. "Poisonous plants and animals". *Danger-Use-Beauty-Fan.* Copyright © 2000 TEAM CO07974, THINKQUEST <http://library.thinkquest.org/C007974/1_1ole.htm>.
72. *Medical Encyclopedia.* Medline Plus, A service of the U.S. National Library of Medicine and the National Institutes of Health, www.nlm.nih.gov/medlineplus/ency/imagepages/3079.
73. References used: Danin 1983; Boulos 1983; Weed Management Guide, White weeping broom (*Retama raetam*) <http://www.weeds.crc.org.au/documents/wmg_white_weeping.pdf>.
74. References used: Vogt 1995; Boulos 1999–2005, v. 2.
75. References used: Grieve 1931; Zoghet and Alsheikh 1999.
76. References used: Boulos 1999–2005, v. 2; Springuel 2000.
77. References used: Vincett 1977.
78. Betty A. Lipscombe Vincett (1977) wrote on traditional belief: "At the birth of Christ it is said that all these plants opened and became green again. There is another story that Mary was holding some of these plants in her hand when Christ was born, causing the plant to curl up like a fist."
79. References used: Zoghet and Alsheikh 1999.
80. References used: Täckholm *et al.* 1941; Hoshovsky 2000.
81. Perdue 1958.
82. References used: Täckholm *et al.* 1941; Boulos 1999–2005, v. 4.
83. *Halfa barr* grows best in the south of Egypt and there is also evidence of its healthy growth in Dina Aly's garden near Cairo.
84. Loutfy Boulos in his four-volume *Flora of Egypt* (1999–2005) described 2075 native and naturalized plants known in Egypt.
85. Common everywhere in desert wadis of the Eastern Desert, Red Sea, and Gebel Elba, in oases of the Western Desert, and in the Nile Valley on the edge of cultivation.
86. *Alcea rosea* is widely cultivated throughout the world. In Egypt it now only grows in Sinai, but it has not been established whether it is an escape from recent cultivation or if it is native. It has been found in Egypt since ancient times, as indicated by its presence in garlands found in pharaonic tombs (Hamdi 2003).
87. The fresh seeds of *Delonix elata* germinate well without pre-treatment according to Dina Aly, who has succeeded in growing young plants in the plant nursery of her desert garden in the Oraby district near Cairo.
88. Marwan El Azzouni grows *Caralluma acutangula* (best known by its old name *Caralluna retrospiciens)* in his garden in Giza.

Bibliography

Abu Al-Izz, M.S. 1971. *Landforms of Egypt*. Cairo: The American University in Cairo Press.

Advisory Committee on Technology Innovation (*ad hoc* panel). 1980. *Firewood Crop, shrubs and trees species for energy production*, Report. Washington D.C.: National Academy of Science.

Alkire, B. 1998. "Capers New Crop factSHEET." Center for New Crop & Plant Products, Purgue University, www.hort.purgue.edu./newcrop//crop-factsheet/caper.html.

El Azzouni, M. 2003. "Conserving *Dracaena ombet*, Egypt's Dragon tree," *Plant Talk* 34: 38–39.

Bainbridge, D.A. 2001. "Buried clay pot irrigation: a little known but very efficient traditional method of irrigation," *Agricultural Water Management* 48: 79–88.

Ball, John. 1900. *Geological Survey Report 1899. Kharga Oasis: Its topography and geology*. Cairo: National Printing Department.

———. 1912. *The Geography and Geology of South-Eastern Egypt*. Cairo: Survey Department.

Belal, A.E., B. Leith, J.Solway and I.Springuel. 1988. *Environmental valuation and management of plants in Wadi Allaqi, Egypt*. Report, International Development Research Center (IDRC) Canada. Aswan: Unit of Environmental Studies and Development (UESD), South Valley University.

Belal, A.E. and Springuel, I. 1996. "Economic Value of Plant Diversity in Arid Environments," *Nature & Resources* 32 (1): 33–39.

Belal, A. and Springuel I. 1997. *Wadi Allaqi Biosphere Reserve*, Brochure. Aswan: Unit of Environmental Studies and Development (UESD), South Valley University.

Bircher, Warda H. 1995. *The Date Palm–A Friend and Companion of Man*, Cairo: Elias Modern Publishing House.

Bornkamm, R. and Kehl, H. 1989. "Landscape ecology of the western desert of Egypt," *Journal of Arid Environments* 17: 271–77.

Bornkamm, R., Springuel I., Darius F., Sheded M.G., and Radi M. 2000. "Some observations on the plant communities of Dungul Oasis (Western Desert, Egypt)," *Acta Botanica Croatia* 59 (1): 101–109.

Boulos, Loutfy. 1968. "The discovery of Medemia palm in the Nubian desert of Egypt," *Botaniska Notiser* 121: 117–20.

———. 1983. *Medicinal Plants of North Africa*. Michigan: Reference publications, Inc.

———. 1999–2005. *Flora of Egypt*, 4 vols. Cairo: Al Hadara Publishing.

Boulos, L. and Barakat, H. 1998. "Some aspects of the plant life in the Western Desert of Egypt," *Journal of Union of Arab Biologists (Cairo)* 5(B): 79–94.

Corner, E.J.H. 1966. *The Natural History of Palms*. London: Weidenfeld and Nicolson.

Dalrymple Belgrave, C. 1922. *Siwa–The Oasis of Jupiter Ammon*. London: John Lane; London: Darf Publishers [undated reprint].

Danin, Avinoam. 1983. *Desert Vegetation of Israel and Sinai*. Israel: Cana Publishing House.

El-Emary, N. and Springuel, I. 1993. "Medicinal Plants in Wadi Allaqi," Assiut, Egypt: *Proceedings of the First National Symposium on Herbal Medicine*: 9–17.

Evans, Dale O. 1994. "NFT Highlights," NFTA 94-06, June 1994, Forest, Farm, and Community Tree Network FACT Net, USA, http://v1.winrock.org/forestry/factpub/factsh/sesban.htm.

Fernandes, Dr. Erick C. M. 2003. *Trees and Shrubs Archive: 'Sesbania sesban (Linn.) Merrill.'* Ithaca: International Agroforestry Resources, Cornell University, www.css.cornell.edu/ecf3/Web/new/AF/treeSsesban.html.

Francis, Raymond. 1998. *The Olive Oil Scandal*. California: Beyond Health, http://www.living-foods.com/articles/oliveoil.html.

Giman, E.F. and Watson, D.G. 1994. *Nerium oleander, Oleander Fact sheet ST-412*, Environmental Horticultural Department, Institute of Food and Agricultural Science, University of Florida, http://hort.ifas.ufl.edu/trees/NEROLEA.pdf.

Gothein, Marie-Luise. 1913. *A History of Garden Art.* Edited, revised, and encoded for copyright protection ©Tom Turner 2000: http://www.gardenvisit.com/got/index.htm.

Grieve, M. 1931. *A Modern Herbal.* Botanical.com. ©1995–2005, http://botanical.com/botanical/mgmh/s/senna-42.html.

Guinand and Lemessa. 2001. *Ethiopia: Famine Food Field Guide, Category 3: Wild Food Plants Attracting Additional Consumer categories.* Addis Ababa: UN-EUE, http://www.africa.upenn.edu/faminefood/category3/Cat3_Injet_tree.htm.

el-Hadidi, Nabil M. and Boulos, Loutfy. 1989. *The Street Trees of Egypt.* Cairo: The American University in Cairo Press.

Hall, J.B. 1992. "Ecology of a key African multipurpose tree species, *Balanites aegyptiaca* (Balanitaceae): the state-of-knowledge," *Forest Ecology and Management* 50: 1–30.

Hamdi, Rim S. 2003. *Documentary and Ethnobotanical studies of floral bouquets and garlands in Egypt since the 18th Dynasty* (Ph.D. Thesis). Cairo: Cairo University.

Hartmann, Hudson T., Kester, Dale E. and Davies, Fred T., Jr. 1990. *Plant Propagation, Principles and Practices.* New Jersey: Prentice-Hall International Inc.

Hepper, Nigel F. 1990. *Pharaoh's Flowers, The Botanical Treasures of Tutankhamun.* London: HMSO, Royal Botanic Gardens, Kew.

Hoshovsky, Marc. 2000. "Element Stewardship Abstract for *Arundo donax,*" *The Global Invasive Species Initiative* ©The Nature Conservancy, update 2005, http://tncweeds.ucdavis.edu/esadocs/arundona.html.

Jarvis, C.S. 1947. *Three Deserts.* London: John Murray.

Johnson, Eric A. and Harbison, David G. 1995. *Lush and Efficient: A Guide to Coachella Valley Landscaping.* California: Coachella Valley Water District. (www.cvwd.org/lush&eff/lsh&ef34.htm).

Krzywinski, Knut. 2001. "Culture Landscapes," in K. Krzywinski and R. H. Pierce, eds., *Deserting the Desert.* Norway: Alvheim & Eide Akademisk Forlag.

Manniche, Lise. 1999 (revised reprint). *An Ancient Egyptian Herbal.* London: British Museum Press.

Miller, Anthony G. and Morris, Miranda. 1988. *Plants of Dhofar. The southern region of Oman, traditional, economic and medicinal uses.* Sultanate of Oman: Diwan of Royal Court, The Office of the Adviser for Conservation of the Environment.

National Academy of Sciences. 1979. *Tropical Legumes: Resources for the future*. Washington, D.C.: National Academy of Sciences.

O'Hara, S.A. "Mediterranean climate gardening throughout the world," www. Mediterraneangardensociety.org/plants/Capparis.spinosa.

Paver, M.A. and Pretorius, D.A. 1954. *Report on hydrological investigations in Kharga and Dakhla oases*. Egypt: L'Institut du Desert d'Egypte.

Perdue, R.E. 1958. "Arundo donax–source of musical reeds and industrial cellulose," *Economic Botany* 12 (4): 368–404.

Rzóska, Julian, ed. 1976. *The Nile, Biology of an Ancient River*. The Hague: W. Junk B.V.

Sahni, K.C. 1968. *Important trees of the Northern Sudan*. Khartoum: United Nations Development Programme and FAO Project.

Sampsell, Bonnie M. 2003. *A Traveler's Guide to the Geology of Egypt*. Cairo: The American University in Cairo Press.

Shaheen, Abdel-Samia Moustafa. 1995. *Morphological and cytogenetical variations in the ecological populations of Acacia species in Egypt*. (Ph.D. Thesis). Assiut: Assiut University, Faculty of Science.

Smit, Nico. 1999. *Guide to the Acacias of South Africa*. South Africa: Briza Publications.

Soliman, Mohamed and Amer, Wafaa. 2002. *Atlas–Trees & Flowers Maadi District*. Cairo: Published by the authors.

Springuel, Irina. 1981. *Studies on Natural Vegetation of the Islands of the First Cataract*. (Ph.D. Thesis). Assiut: Assiut University.

———. 2000. *Cultivation of medicinal plants. Solenostemma arghel*, Brochure. Aswan: Unit of Environmental Studies and Development.

———. 2001. "Indigenous Agroforestry for sustainable development of the area around Lake Nasser, Egypt." In S. W. Breckle, M. Veste, W. Wucherer, eds., *Sustainable Land Use in Deserts*. Berlin and Heidelberg: Springer-Verlag.

Springuel, I. and Mekki, A.M. 1994. "Economic value of desert plants: *Acacia* trees in Wadi Allaqi Biosphere Reserve." *Environmental Conservation* 21 (1): 41–48.

Springuel, I., Faraldi, C., Ibrahim, H., Hamed, N. 2005. "Biological diversity and material culture in Siwa Oasis" (Report). Cairo: UNESCO.

Suttie, J.M. 2005. "Grassland Species Profiles," Sesbania sesban (L.) Merr, http://www.fao.org/ag/AGP/AGPC/doc/Gbase/DATA/Pf000170.HTM.

Täckholm, Vivi. 1974. *Students' Flora of Egypt*. Cairo: Cairo University.

———. 1976. "Ancient Egypt, landscape, flora and agriculture," in

Täckholm, Gunnar F., Täckholm, Vivi, and Drar, Mohmmed. 1941. "Flora of Egypt Vol.1," *Bulletin of the Faculty of Science* No.17. Cairo: Fouad I University.

Täckholm, Vivi and Drar, Mohammed. 1950. "Flora of Egypt Vol. II," *Bulletin of the Faculty of Science* No. 28. Cairo: Fouad I University.

The Aircav® Survival-Appendix B, Edible and medicinal plants, http://www.aircav.com/survival/appb/asappbtoc.html

Verdcourt, Bernard and Trump, E.C. 1969. *Common Poisonous Plants of East Africa*. London: Collins.

Vincett, Betty A. Lipscombe. 1977. *Wild Flowers of Central Saudi Arabia*. Milan: Published by the author.

Vivian, Cassandra. 2000. *The Western Desert of Egypt*. Cairo: The American University in Cairo Press.

Vogt, Kees. 1995. *A Field Worker's Guide to the Identification, Propagation and Uses of Common Trees and Shrubs of Dryland Sudan*. London: SOS Sahel International (UK).

Wilkinson, Alix. 1998. *The Garden in Ancient Egypt*. London: Rubicon Press.

Zahran, M.A. and Willis, A.J. 1992. *Vegetation of Egypt*. London: Chapman & Hall.

Zoghet, Mouin F. and Alsheikh, Abdulmalick A. 1999. *Wild Plants in the Region of Riyadh*. Riyadh: King Saud University, Academic Publishing and Press.

Zohary, Daniel and Hopf, Maria. 1988. *Domestication of Plants in the Old World*. Oxford: Clarendon Press.

Index

Numbers in **bold** *refer to plates in the color section*

Abu Simbel xiv–xv, 17
Abutilon pannosum 139
Acacia albida 64, 66, 83
Acacia arabica 16, 41, 143
Acacia ehrenbergiana 3, 13, 35, 42,
    54, 65–66, 68, 69–70, **1**
Acacia laeta 16, 35, 41, 45–46,
    64–66, 68–69, 71, **2**
Acacia mellifera 66, 68, 72–73, **3**
Acacia nilotica 13, 32, 41, 46, 54, 65,
    66, 69, 74, **4**
Acacia pachyceras 36, 42, 64–66, 77,
    145, **5**
Acacia seyal 31, 35, 41, 43, 64, 66,
    77–78, **6**
Acacia tortilis subsp. *raddiana* 3, 13,
    16, 35, 42, 65–66, 81, **8**
Acacia tortilis subsp. *tortilis* 3, 35,
    42, 65–66, 79, 80, **7**
agol 11, 13
agram 6
al-Alamein xiv
Alcea apterocarpa 139
Alcea rosea 139, 147
Alcea striata 139
Alexandrian senna 128
Anabasis articulata 6, 141

Anastatica hierochuntica 19, 24, 35,
    45–46, 132–33, **33**
angel's trumpet 134
Anticharis arabica 6
Anticharis linearis 6
apple ring acacia 35–36, 50, 64, 83
araak 100, 146
argel 129
argoun xv, 14, 25–26, 32, 40, 42, 46,
    54, 113–14, 146
al-Arish 115, 135
arta 7, 27, 31, 45, 117–19
Arundo donax 15, 28, 135–37,
    150–51, **35**
Aswan High Dam Lake 16, 35
atel 104
athel 104
athl 104
Australian pine xiv

al-baan 96
Bahariya 7
Balanites aegyptiaca 4, 13, 32, 41,
    46, 85, 144, 150, **10**
Baris 13, 87
Birket Maraqi 9
Birket Siwa 9
Birket Zaytun 9
bulrushes 11

153

Calligonum comosum 31
Calligonum polygonoides 7, 27, 45,
  117–18, **25**
Calotropis procera 32, 42, 88–89, **11**
caper xv, 26, 31, 46, 119–20
Capparis decidua 4, 21 46, 90, **12**
Capparis spinosa 26, 31, 119–20,
  146, 151, **26**
Caralluma acutangula 144, 147
Cassia senna 6
castor oil plant 25, 32, 35, 38, 41,
  126–27
casuarina xiv–xv
Ceratonia siliqua 140
Christ-thorn 4, 26, 30, 36, 44–45,
  107, 146
Cleome chrysantha 6
Cleome droserifolia 6
Cleome paradoxa 6
Convolvulus oleifolius 140
Convolvulus dorycnium 140
Convolvulus hystrix 140
Convolvulus lanatus 140
Convolvulus scammonia 140
Cotula cinerea 6
Crataegus azarolus 140
Crataegus sinaica 140
Cymbopogon proximus 2, 24, 39,
  40–41, 137
Cymbopogon schoenanthus subsp.
  proximus 137–38, **36**
Cyperus papyrus 15

Dakhla 7, 151
Damietta 15
date palm xvii, 10, 13, 16, 29, 30,
  32–33, 44, 49, 115, 117
datura 134
Datura innoxia 15, 32, 35, 42, 46,
  134–35, **34**
Delonix elata 140, 144, 147
Delonix regia 140

desert date 85
Desmostachya bipinnata 14
difla 122
Dineigil Oasis 13
Dodonaea viscosa 141
doum palm 14, 16, 25–26, 30–33, 42,
  45–46, 48–49, 111, 113
downy thorn apple xvii, 15, 29, 32,
  35, 46, 134
Draceana ombet 109, 144, **21**
Dungul Oasis 13–14, 113, 143

Egyptian plum xv, 4–5, 13, 17,
  22–23, 26, 30–32, 36, 41, 46, 49,
  85, 88
Egyptian rattle pod 102
Egyptian sycomore 91
Egyptian thorn 74
Eucalyptus trees xiv
Euphorbia consobrina
Euphorbia dendroides 141
Euphorbia consobrina 141
Euphorbia polyacantha 140
Fagonia indica 6
Faidherbia albida 16, 35–36, 40–41,
  46, 64–66, 83, **9**
Farafra 7
Fayoum 7
Ficus carica 32
Ficus sycomorus 23, 32, 37, 91–92,
  13
First Cataract Islands 16, 41, 46, 71,
  72, 77, 79, 84

Gebel Elba xvi, 23, 64, 71–72, 74, 79.
  85, 90, 93–94, 96, 100, 109–10,
  128, 132, 139, 140–41, 144, 147
Gebel Uweinat 7
ghaab baladi 135
ghaab rumi 135
ghadha 93
giant reed 28, 31, 135–36

Gilf Kebir 7
gimmeiz 91
Gisekia pharnaceoides 6
Glaucium grandiflorum 139

haashab 72
habriga 90
halfa barr 5, 40–41, 46, 48, 137–38
Haloxylon persicum 6, 21, 24, 31, 46, 93
Haloxylon salicornicum 6, 94, 141
hand of the Virgin Mary's flower 132
haraz 83
hargal 5, 17, 25, 27, 31, 36, 41, 46, 129–30
hashaab 71
heglik 85
Hibiscus vitifolius 139
hommad 5
hook thorn 72
horseradish tree 26, 32, 46, 96
Hyoscyamus muticus 42
Hyphaene thebaica 14, 32, 38, 42, 110–113, **22**

Imperata cylindrical 14, 138
Indian Laurel xiv–xv, 32
Ipomoea pes-caprae 140

Jasminum fluminense subsp. *gratissimum* 140
Jasminum grandiflorum subsp. *floribundum* 140
Juncus rigidus 9, 13
Juniperus phoenicea 141

kabbar 119
kaff mariam 132
Kalabsha 17
kamoaab 94
khaaraz 83
Kharga Oasis 9, 12–13, 85–87, 105

kharwa 126
kitr 72

Lake Nasser xv, 35, 65, 74, 83, 104, 151
laloob 85
Lantana camara 140
Lantana viburnoides 140
lassaf 119
Leptadenia arborea 16
Leptadenia pyrotechnica 121–22, 144, **27**
Lupinus digitatus 6

Maerua crassifolia 4, 94–95, **14**
marekh, markh 121
Medemia argun 8, 14–15, 23, 32, 42, 46, 113–14, 143, **23**
Mimosa pigra 16
miswaak 100
Moringa peregrina 21–22, 24, 26, 32, 46, 96–97, 144, **15**
mulberry fig 91
mustard tree 100–101

nabaq 107
Nakhila Oasis 14, 113
nakhla al-balah 115
Nerium oleander 122–23, 149, **28**
Nile acacia 15–16, 26, 31–32, 44–45, 74–75
Nubian dragon tree 109–10
Nymphaea lotus 15

Olea chrysophylla 23
Olea europaea 32, 97–99, 140
olive xvii, 9–10, 30, 32, 36, 44, 97–99, 140, **16**
oleander xvii, 23, 29, 32, 36, 44, 122–124
ombeit 109
oshar 88

Pavonia hirsuta 139
Persian reed 135
Phoenix dactylifera 10, 14, 23,
   32–33, 38, 115–16, **24**
Pistacia 32, 141
Pluchea dioscoridis 16
Pulicaria incise 6, 42

retam, retem 124
Red Sea Hills 2, 4, 72, 79, 94, 109,
   128, 141
Retama monosperma 125
Retama raetam 7, 21, 45, 124–25,
   144, **30**
Ricinus communis 32, 41, 126–27, **31**
Rosa arabica 140
rose of Jericho 19, 35, 45–46, 48–49,
   132

saarh 94
saisaban 16, 38, 102
salam 3, 69
salamekki 128
Saluga and Ghazel 4, 46, 72, 79
Salvadora persica 4, 46, 100–101, **17**
samoor 79
sant, sont 74
sayaal 77, 81
selem 69
senna 47, 128–29
Senna alexandrina 6, 24, 42, 47,
   128–29, **29**
Senna italica 6
senna mekki 128
Sesamum alatum 6
sesban 102
Sesbania sesban 38, 42, 102–103, **18**
shaay gabali 6
sidr 107
Siwa Oasis 7, 9, 10–12, 99, 142
siwaak 100

Sodom apple 29, 32, 35, 48, 106
Solenostemma arghel 31, 41, 46, 48,
   129–31, **32**
sycomore fig 26, 30, 32, 34–38,
   44–45, 91–92, 143

tagart bush 4, 94
talh 77
tamarisk xv, 5, 9, 11, 14, 16, 17, 21,
   26, 29, 31, 34–38, 40, 44–45, 54,
   104–105
Tamarix aphylla 21, 29, 31, 37, 42,
   54, 104–105, **19**
Tamarix nilotica 5, 42
tatura 134
tekkeer 72
toothbrush tree xv, 4–5, 46, 100
toundoub 90

umbrella thorn 3, 4, 79

Wadi Allaqi xiii, xvii, 4–5, 17, 39,
   58–59, 61–62, 83, 85, 91, 100, 131,
   142–44
Wadi Gemal 4
Wadi Haimur 5
Wadi Natrun 7
Wadi Qena 5
wait a bit thorn 72
ward el himar 122
white acacia 26, 40, 49, 64, 83
white broom 7, 27, 31, 45, 124–25
white saksaul 6, 21, 24, 31, 46, 49,
   93–94
white weeping broom 124

yasaar 96

zaitoun 97
Ziziphus spina-christi 4, 16, 32,
   42–43, 107, **20**